UNPACKING
MEMORIES

THE STORY OF A SUITCASE,
A COUNTRY DOCTOR,
& A COMMUNITY

UNPACKING MEMORIES

THE STORY OF A SUITCASE,
A COUNTRY DOCTOR,
& A COMMUNITY

DEBORAH SWEANEY

WORD ASSOCIATION PUBLISHERS
www.wordassociation.com
1.800.827.7903

This book is dedicated to my mom, Iris McCluey Sweaney.
Without her strength, perseverance and faith, this story would not
have been possible.

These memories are for Carry who was too young to remember.

ISBN: 978-1-59571-848-8

Library of Congress Control Number: 2012921891

Designed and published by
Word Association Publishers
205 Fifth Avenue
Tarentum, Pennsylvania 15084

www.wordassociation.com

1.800.827.7903

TABLE OF CONTENTS

Appreciation 9

Preface 11

Going Home 13

    You Look Like Iris 20

    Debby, Let's Go Waste Some Money 22

A Love Story 25

    I Guess You Know We Are Going To Be Married When I
    Return 27

Holt County, 1952 41

    How All Has Been Changed by The Hand of Progress! 43

    I Don't Need Any Money. I'll Put It On The Sweaney Tab. 49

    A River With A Personality 55

Health Care (Fifties Style) 61

    Kid, That First Day Doc Was Busy, Busy; You Might Say
    Swamped 63

    No One Ever Called Her "Anna." 67

    I Remember Your Home. It Was Where We Went If We Were
    Sick and Your Dad's Office Was Closed 70

    I Can Make A Living Delivering Kurtz Babies 72

    You Could Set Your Clock By Doc Sweaney 74

    Doc Sweaney Was A Country Doctor, But He Did Not Have
    A Horse And Buggy. Doc Had An Oldsmobile 76

    If I Hadn't Gone On House Calls, I Might Never Have Seen
    Him 79

    Four Hours, Four Calls, Four Counties 84

Doc Sweaney Gave A Pint Of Blood Directly From His Own
Body 85

The Doctors There Are Really On The Ball! 88

Doc Sweaney Delivered Me 92

Oregon's March Of Dimes 99

I Relied On Just Ten Drugs. Two Of Them Were Cough
Syrup and Aspirin 106

Life In Rural America 111

I Can't Imagine What Mom and Dad Went Through at That
Time. 113

We Were Guided and Encouraged. 119

Everyone Could Tell You Where The Sweaneys Lived. .. 126

Dick Said, "Here, Spot! Come And Get This. This Is For You
Run, Spot, Run. 131

Look! Up In The Sky! 135

It was "I before E except after C." 137

King James and Uncle Sam Lived Side by Side. 144

The Month of May, 1960. 148

Everything Changes 151

Betty Millison Called. 153

I See Snapshots In My Mind. 158

Pretty Hard Year. 163

Epilogue 173

Notes 179

About the Author 183

APPRECIATION

This book belongs to the people of Holt County, Missouri. Thank you for welcoming me back into your hearts and your homes. Your stories and pictures made this book possible. I cannot begin to name everyone who shared memories with me. If I try, I will just leave a name off the list and offend someone. If I missed a few details or my memory is different than yours, please forgive me. I hope that I captured the times in which we lived.

I do want to mention the physicians who shared their memories of practicing medicine at that time: Dr. Wallace Carpenter, Dr. Jay Milne, Dr. John Wanamaker, and Dr. Harold Kretzing. You helped me understand my father's life and illness. A special thanks to Ann Schlueter for opening the doors of the old Fairfax Hospital to me. It was wonderful sharing memories with the women who worked with my parents more than fifty years ago: Yvonne Lippold Markt, Pat Kee Pekarek, Phyllis Narans, and Evelyn Matthews Yeary.

I appreciate the encouragement of my friends and family as I tried to develop my new narrative skills. The two Jim's in my life (my husband and my brother) and my friend Cathy Gorn read my early writings and offered suggestions. Helen Walker, a Messiah College English professor, reviewed my draft and shared her expertise. I also want to extend my special thanks to Rev. Bruce Stevens, Synod of the Trinity, for his coaching and affirmation. Furthermore, I now know why authors frequently acknowledge their editors; mine, Cynthia Nelson, made this the book I wanted it to be.

My love goes to my siblings, Lou Ann, Jim, and Carry. Mom and Dad did a pretty good job when they created us. This book is also for Kelly Atkins Kurtz, Mom's other daughter. It has been wonderful sharing this journey into another time with you. Of course, there is my husband, Jim Baker. He has adapted his "city ways" for me. I cherish him.

Preface

Time travel is one of our fantasies. If we could just go back in time, just re-live those moments when the world changed, then maybe we could somehow make it all right. My fantasies can become elaborate: I could be in the stairway of the Texas Book Depository on November 22, 1963 and trip Lee Harvey as he runs up to his assassination lair on the sixth floor, or warn Frederick Fleet in time to stop the Titanic from running into the iceberg. My fantasies, however, are nothing more than that—flights of fancy. We cannot change the past, but we can revisit it.

This past year I did engage in a type of time travel. I journeyed back in time to the years between 1952 and 1960 when my father practiced medicine in a small town in Northwest Missouri. I left 2012 behind and the black and white photos of my youth came alive. But, I went further than that. I travelled back to my home town of Oregon, Missouri and spoke with people who knew and loved my dad, Doc Sweaney, and who shared a bond with our family. And yet, as I revisited the events of those years, I did so with a new set of eyes – no longer, the eyes of a long-legged, barely eight year old little girl, but the eyes of a woman who had just turned sixty.

Still, I could not make it all right. I could not change the events of the summer of 1960. I could not extend Dad's life beyond his time or alter the incredible sadness of his death.

My father's life ended before the events of the tumultuous sixties, before the Great Society programs, or the Vietnam War. He died before Medicare changed the way doctors are paid and before the Interstate Highway system reached Holt County and changed transportation routes. He died not seeing the many advances in health care that we take for granted, some of which might even have benefited his own health—his obesity, hypertension, and the possible diabetes that resulted in his kidneys failing would have been treated differently today.

But no, the summer of 1960 happened. Dad died.

Just as I always knew; there is no changing the past. But now I understand it, and consequently, I also understand myself a little better.

GOING HOME

My journey starts with a suitcase. My grandmother's suitcase was cheaply made and not really the best receptacle in which to store important family memorabilia. It let in moisture. When I opened it in January 2012, moldy air wafted through the room. I don't know what I expected to find, but I was transported to the most important month of my life, July 1960. It was the month I turned eight. It was the month that both my father and my grandfather died. I returned to a time and place that is no more, to a small town in Northwest Missouri in the 1950s.

After my mom's death in 1989, I gathered with my siblings, Lou Ann, Jim, and Carry, to clean out her house and to divide up family possessions. After a week of cleaning and sorting, I had reduced my memories to a small pile of physical reminders waiting to be loaded into a commercial moving van. Since they did not begin to reach the freight minimum, I looked around for some other items to send to my home in the Washington D.C. suburbs. I added Grandma McCluey's suitcase to the stack.

I stored it, unopened, in the back of a closet, in the back of my mind. Twenty-two years after Mom's funeral, I stumbled over the old brown metal suitcase while putting away some Christmas decorations. It was rusted in spots, the red stripe around its center still visible, but the cloth handle had long ago rotted. I became curious, moved it upstairs from my basement to my guest bedroom, and opened it.

It was full of greeting cards, get-well messages sent to my father when he was in the hospital, and sympathy cards sent to my mother after his death, packed away fifty-two years earlier in that hot summer of 1960.

My father, Dr. Frank Sweaney, was a mythic figure who dominated my childhood. My memories of him were fixed in time, formed through a child's eyes. These cards moved him beyond the limits of my childhood awareness. His life and its impact became real.

In my obsessive way, I counted the cards, dividing them into two stacks. One stack for get-well cards, the other for cards sent in sympathy. There were over a thousand, almost evenly divided. I started examining the get-well cards. Many were still in envelopes, with postmarks from June and July, 1960. They were addressed to a hospital room in Missouri Methodist Hospital in St. Joseph, the room where Dad died.

At first, they seemed like nothing more than interesting historic artifacts. The humor was so different from today's humor. Many carried religious messages and several had pictures of Jesus on them. I started examining the signatures. Almost all were signed by more than one name: a husband and wife, and frequently the names of their children. Several of the cards had a list of signatures on them. I closed my eyes and could see the card and pen being passed from hand to hand along a church pew or at a community meeting. I recognized many of the names and my memory formed fuzzy pictures of faces. It was, however, the number of names that amazed me. We lived in such a small community. Oregon, Missouri, had only 800 people, the entire Holt County approximately 6,000. There were over 1,200 signatures on the cards.

I started reading. Repeatedly, I saw the words, "Just rest up and come back to us. We need you." People wrote of their ailments and family concerns. It irked me a little that they seemed more concerned with their needs than his condition. Did they not know he was dying? What did they think was happening to him? He had been in the hospital for a month before he died. Did they not realize how very sick he was? I felt an incredible sadness and more than a little anger over his untimely death at age forty.

I turned to the sympathy cards. Over and over I read messages such as, "It is hard to imagine that God just needed Doc more than we did." Or, "He can rest now." My anger returned, more intense: There is no way in heaven God needed my dad more than his wife and four small children did.

Seated on the floor of my guest room in central Pennsylvania, holding cards sent more than half a century earlier, I grieved, not just for my father and my mother, but for that small, brown-eyed, little girl whose life was so irrevocably changed that summer. I missed the man that I knew only through sketchy childhood memories. Fifty-two years after my dad's death, I decided to return to our tiny community, to the land of my childhood. I needed to know Dad as a person, to see him as an adult.

I sent an open letter to the local Oregon, Missouri paper notifying people that I would be visiting to gather memories. The response was overwhelming—a barrage of e-mails, phone calls, and letters from people telling me stories about Dad. I arranged reunions and luncheons. People that I had not seen for forty years wrote me and invited me to stay in their homes.

Three months after opening Grandma McCluey's battered suitcase, I landed at the Kansas City International Airport. It took me a moment to get my bearings. The airport is north of the city in the middle of what was once farmland. As I drove, I recognized landmarks and memories returned. I was going home for the first time in twenty-three years. I decided to leave the interstate and take old Highway 59 north. As I crossed the border into Holt County I thought, this is the road Mom and Dad would have taken almost sixty years ago when they first came to Oregon, and my mom would have been pregnant with me.

I had allotted five days for my visit. I lived five decades in those five days. I talked with people who knew Dad. I travelled the roads that he had travelled to visit his patients. Those "decades" didn't diminish the pain of my dad's death, but they provided me with an opportunity to face it as an adult. In doing so, I was able to reclaim the joy and innocence of the time before that day in July, 1960, when he died.

We were raised on stories about my dad. These stories kept him alive in a way, an active part of our family life long after he was gone. Now, after so many years, I was listening to people tell me their stories about my dad. His life and death were part of their personal narratives. He was a bit of a character and the stories sometimes sounded a little exaggerated. At first I tried to separate fact from myth, but I came to the conclusion that it was not worth the effort. The stories captured people's feelings about Dad, including their sadness and grief from the summer of 1960.

While opening the suitcase brought back the sadness of that summer, hearing the stories of friends, neighbors, former patients, and colleagues shifted my focus from mourning his death to appreciating his life. So, if the occasional detail is less than absolutely accurate, if the events happened a little differently, it really doesn't matter. These are the stories of my parents: their love story, the story of the life they created, and the story of the community where they lived. Some are warm and funny, others make me sad. Some are based on memories of people who knew and loved my parents. Others are mine, the memories of a little girl who watched these stories happen.

What I knew as family lore grew into a larger story—community lore—and the story of Oregon, Missouri, the county seat of rural Holt County, in the years between 1952 and 1960.

My father could have chosen to practice medicine any place in America. It was this community that he chose to serve with love.

You Look Like Iris.

— Betty Bendure, 2012

I arrived in Oregon on a Saturday afternoon. I drove through the town, looking at the square and the surrounding stores. At first glance it was as I remembered, except for a couple of empty store fronts. I thought the town looked a little tired.

I stopped at a local café, The 275 Grill. Three older women were seated at a round table. Betty Bendure introduced herself and her two companions, Martha O'Connell and Billie Summer. The minute I heard Martha and Billie's names I saw them as they appeared fifty years earlier. Martha's childbirth story was an important part of my family narrative. Billie, my grade school cook, had made wonderful cinnamon rolls.

Betty said, "You must be Debby. You look like Iris." It was a strange feeling to hear those words from someone I did not recognize. Over the next five days those words were frequently repeated. I had never before been told that I looked like my mother. All my life I had been told that I looked like a Sweaney. Sweaneys are larger people. It is not until you stand next to a Sweaney that you realize that we are much shorter than you thought. Sweaneys have short legs (making it hard for me to buy jeans off the rack). We are prone to weight gain.

I liked this new image.

I had not inherited the slight bone structure of women in my mother's family. I was always the largest girl in any family picture. At barely five foot four, I still felt like a giant. McCluey women are short, neat, and tidy. Mom could put on a dress that she bought at a yard sale and look good in it. But you should never be fooled by their small stature. McCluey women have backbones.

Dad was never neat and tidy, always looking a little mussed. He needed someone to follow after him to make sure that his shirt tail was tucked into his pants, and that his latest snack was not on his white shirt. He was lucky, not only did he have Mom to tidy him up, he had a large staff of women who helped keep him in order.

It was memories of my parents that had brought me back to Missouri, and now my presence was bringing back memories of both Iris and Frank Sweaney to the three women in the café.

I pictured Dad and Mom. Not only did my parents differ in their appearance, but a child's tea set bought during the Holt County Fall Festival fifty-three years earlier has come to symbolize another difference.

DEBBY, LET'S GO
WASTE SOME MONEY.
— Dad, 1959

Each year in September, Oregon, Missouri is host to the Holt County Fall Festival. The town plans the fair for months. The excitement begins to build on Labor Day when the Kiwanis food tent goes up close to the Courthouse. Only a select few of the town leaders know the secret recipe for their ranch burgers. Women in town are drafted to make home-made pies to complement the burgers. Church basements and community rooms are turned over to the fair and the best preserves, knitted items, and quilts are arranged, judged, and put on display. Tents on the square house prize-winning local produce.

For the children in town, Wednesday of Fair Week holds a special excitement as the carnival trucks roll into town and the roustabouts set up the midway on the west side of the town square. The Junior Queen Contest is held early on Thursday night followed by the Senior Queen Contest. The parade on Saturday afternoon features floats built by community organizations that hope their creative efforts will win a coveted prize. The parade starts on the edge of town as marching bands from area schools, antique cars, floats, and the queen and her attendants in convertibles proceed slowly to the town square. The route is crowded with citizens sitting on lawn chairs.

The tradition of the Fall Festival began in 1952, the year my parents moved to the community. The parade and the queen contests, which are now the preeminent events of the weekend, were first held the following year. Gary Kurtz brought his camera to the parade that year. His pictures throughout this book illustrate life in Holt County in the 1950s. Many of the advertisements that capture the spirit of the business community are from the Fall Festival brochures from the period.

Yvonne Lippold, right, as an attendant in the first Fall Festival Queen Contest, 1953. (Courtesy of Gary Kurtz)

At the 1959 fair, I was seven. My mother always gave my sister and me (her eldest children) a dollar for each fair day. This dollar bought a day of entertainment and an incredible freedom of choice. We could buy four carnival rides, risk it on the games of chance in the midway, or buy cotton candy or other sugar-laden treats.

By the afternoon when my mother came to take us home, I, of course, had already spent the precious dollar. But I was not ready to leave. As many children might, I started crying. Mom staunchly led us through the midway to Dad's office. The Octopus, the largest, and what seemed to me the most dangerous carnival ride, sat directly in front of his door. (In my child's eyes, this felt appropriate. If someone was thrown off this scary ride, they would have immediate medical help.)

By the time we entered my father's office, my tears couldn't be missed. I can still see my father coming out of his examining room with a stethoscope around his neck. Immediately he said, "Debby, why are you crying?"

I answered, "Because, Mommy won't let me waste money."

He just laughed, took my hand and said, "Debby, let's go waste some money." He took me up the street to Scheib's Hardware. There we bought a child's tea set. I now realize that he was having fun not only with my childish statement but with my mother. Even though my father's medical practice was thriving, she protested frivolous spending.

My father died before the next festival. The two pieces of the tea set that remain are two of my most treasured possessions.

A LOVE STORY

I Guess You Know We Are Going To Be Married When I Return.

—Frank Sweaney, 1945

My parent's love story began in the Ozark Mountains of Missouri in the first part of the twentieth century. My father's family was full of funny and fun-loving romantic figures. The McClueys never seemed to have any fun. They worried about keeping the farm, avoiding debt, and conserving what they had.

By the time my mother was born in 1918, the McClueys had lived in America for four generations, but Mom was Scots-Irish to the core. She could stretch a dime until it seemed to be a dollar and wear a pair of panty hose longer than any woman I ever knew. She made us save our bath water to be carried to her garden in buckets. Having lived through the drought of the dust bowl years she chided us, "You never waste water."

Mom's ancestors had fled religious persecution as part of the Scots migration, first to Ireland and then to America. Stories were passed down about McClueys being burned at the stake for their beliefs while chanting the 23rd Psalm. Even now when I hear the words, "Yea, though I walk through the valley of the shadow of death..." I think of my ancestors being burned alive. The McClueys eventually migrated to the Ozark Hills of Dade County, Missouri. Their conservative religious beliefs were passed down through the generations and my mother was raised in this tradition. She told stories of not being able to play games on Sunday, having to sit quietly in God's presence.

Grandma and Grandpa McCluey on their Ozark farm during the depression.

My grandfather, Thomas Finley McCluey, lived most of his life on a section of land in the Ozark foothills where he was born. The family home was little more than a shack without running water or electricity. During the depression, he held three mortgages on the property. My grandfather was an ardent Republican and was passionately opposed to FDR's New Deal. He refused to take what he considered government "charity." The fear of losing the family land was a pressing concern for the family during my mother's early years. She absorbed this fear. Even during the years of my father's successful practice, her apprehension about financial calamity was not buried too deeply under her skin. After my father died, one of her first thoughts was that she would have to take up this worry once more.

The Sweaneys lived another existence. They were mountain folks. Now, we would romantically call them "hillbillies." Granny Sweaney was married when she was fourteen and had my father when she was fifteen. In my family, no one ever counted the months between those two milestones too carefully. My Uncle Woodrow came along soon after my dad was born.

One day Granny was home with just the two small boys. Woodrow was on her hip and Dad was clinging to her skirts, when a stranger came to the door. In the oft repeated story, sometimes he became a "revenuer." For whatever reason, my grandmother did not trust him. She put Uncle Woodrow down on the floor, detached herself from Dad, and took down the shotgun that always hung over the mantel. She aimed, not very precisely, and fired. She only hit the fence post, but the stranger got the message and fled. She told Grandpa about the visitor when he came home. Sweaney men loved the story and told it often.

The Sweaneys have the gift of humor, frequently it is a little irreverent, but never harsh or mean spirited—even subjects of the jokes laugh. It is hard to capture the Sweaney humor in writing since so much of it rests on its delivery. People remember Dad and talk about the "twinkle in his eyes" when he teased— and I know what they mean because the same twinkle glints in my brother's eyes.

The Sweaney Family at the time of the 'shooting story.' Granny is holding Uncle Woodrow, Dad at her side with Grandpa Sweaney on the right.

Uncle Woodrow was a Sweaney through and through. Like many Sweaney men, he played the fiddle. We all loved to be around him. Last year I received a gift of pictures from my dad's family. One of them was a class picture taken in front of a one-room school. The two Sweaney boys, clad in overalls, are in the front row. The picture captures their different spirits. Uncle Woodrow is standing with his arms akimbo, displaying "attitude." Dad, beside him, looks reserved and serious. Family members have said that Dad always had his nose in a book. It is not hard to pick out which of the boys will be the first member of his family to graduate from high school and later college and medical school.

Woodrow and Frank Sweaney, the last two boys on the front row, outside their one-room school.

The Sweaneys never owned farm land. The depression truly did not hit them that hard. As my Uncle Woodrow once said, "we never had had any money," so the depression that rocked the country during the thirties did not alter their lives. Unlike my mother's experience, the Great Depression was not the formative force of my father's childhood.

When my father was stationed overseas in the army during World War II, Grandma Sweaney published his address in the local paper and asked anyone who knew him to write to him. Since they had shared seats on the school bus, Mom may have begun the letters out of a feeling of patriotic duty, but they soon turned into love letters. Lou Ann and I joked about the letter in which Dad wrote, "I guess

Dad walking sentry duty in Panama during World War II. He wrote Mom the letter on the next pages from Panama. Mom was teaching in a one-room school.

you know we are going to be married when I return..." He never even asked her! Yet they were married in December 1945 after my father's return from the service.

Iris and Frank Sweaney spent their wedding night in Springfield, Missouri. They wanted to drive to Kansas City but that would have meant a night together before the wedding. Grandfather McCluey vetoed that idea. After the wedding, my father resumed his studies at the University of Missouri in Columbia. He had made it to college before the war on a small agriculture scholarship. Now, with the GI Bill, Dad could focus on his dream to become a country doctor. He became the recipient of what inadvertently was the most successful social reengineering program in our country's history.

My mother quickly became my father's helpmate and strength. She put aside her own education to focus on his.

Frank and Iris Sweaney on the day of their wedding. The war is over and anything is possible. They look so happy. Dad appears tanned after service in Panama.

Company D. 150th Infantry
A.P.O. 827 c/o Postmaster
New Orleans, Louisiana
January 4, 1945.

Dear Iris,

Certainly sorry to hear that you were sick and hope by now that you are feeling all right again. It is just about the same routine around here from day to day now, so we are getting to the place where we do our jobs almost automatically.

The mention of all that ice and snow on the ground makes me think as if a real Missouri winter has just about setin with you. Some of those sleet storms we used to have when I was walking to high school made me get to the place where I even hate the mere mention of the word ice. Guess you find it hard to keep the school house warm with it so cold. The folks at home burn wood, so dad is usually kept pretty busy keeping it up.

I have got a friend who is attending Louisville Medical school. He was writing me the other day about his experience in the laboratory & he makes me sort of some of the stuff he writes about do

Mom saved Dad's letters. They capture so much of the personal experience of World War II. In reading them, you can feel the growing romance between my parents. The wording, of course, is very circumspect, reflecting both the times and the fact that the letters were subject to military censorship. Dad's letters are written by hand in beautiful cursive script. One of them is reproduced here. Each page is transcribed on an accompanying page to make his words easier to comprehend.

Dear Iris,

Certainly sorry to hear that you were sick and hope by now that you are feeling all right again. It is just about the same routine around here from day to day now so we are getting to the place where we do our jobs almost automatically.

The mention of all that ice and snow on the ground makes me think as if a real Missouri winter has just about set in with you. Some of those sleet storms we used to have when I was walking to high school made me get to the place where I even hate the mention of the word ice. Guess you find it hard to keep the schoolhouse warm with it so cold. The folks at home burn wood, so dad is usually kept pretty busy keeping it up.

I have got a friend who is attending Louisville Medical school, he was writing me the other day about his experiences there in the laboratory and he makes me sort of homesick, some of the stuff he writes about doing, especially his experiments in blood & hormones were the same things I did after finishing at M.U. & it just makes me sort of feel funny to hear him talk about them. Tell of his troubles with them and realize that just a few years back I was doing the same. Oh - well that's the way I guess.

You say you don't deserve a present like the purse. You deserve it and more than I'll ever probably be able to give you, Was glad you liked it. Wish it could of been something better.

Did Avis have any more big tales to tell you when she was home, or was a real "snow storm" enough for her this time? Goldie says she is standing on her head everytime she goes out of the house at home. She'll probably want mother to carry her everytime she goes out of the house.

I haven't been to a show now for about a month. Guess I'm "slipping" usually see most everyone which comes to the theater. It's about the best thing to do in a place like this.

Today has been my day off, I've spent most of it sleeping, so even tonight am still his experiments in blood and hormones were the same things I did after finishing at M.U. and it just makes me sort of feel funny to hear him talk about them. Tell of his troubles with them and recognize that just a few years back I was doing the same. Oh-well that's the way I guess.

You say you don't deserve a present like the purse. You deserve it and more than I'll ever probably be able to give you. Was glad you liked it. Wish it could of been something better.

Did Avis have any more big tales to tell you when she was home, or was a real "snow storm" enough for her this time? Goldie says she is standing on her head every time she goes out of the house at home. She'll probably want mother to carry her every time she goes out of the house.

I haven't been to a show now for about a month. Guess I'm "slipping" usually see most everyone which comes to the theater. It's about the best thing to do in a place like this.

Today has been my day off. I've spent most of it sleeping, so even tonight am still pretty thick headed, guess I'll have to stay up late enough to get awake.

The war news doesn't sound so awfully bad. Perhaps it will be over before so awfully much longer. Quite a few big things are being planned for the soldiers after it is over. Everything from houses for them to an education. I wonder just what it will be like?

Wish I could have been there Christmas. You sound as if everything was pretty nice. I was glad to get your letter so close to the other one. I think letters written more often, although maybe not as long are really best. A person doesn't really know just what a letter can mean. It may not even contain anything of interest, but just the fact that it was a letter means a great deal, especially if that letter is from some one whom the person thinks a great deal of.

Well, I've begun to ramble and you'll be tired of reading this mess. Perhaps I can write a better one next time. Probably I won't sleep all day & will be able to think. So until next I'll keep watching the mail for a letter from you and as ever

Love
Frank.

pretty thick headed, guess I'll have to stay up late enough to get awake.

The war news doesn't sound so awfully bad. Perhaps it will be over before so awfully much longer. Quite a few big things are being planned for the soldiers after it is over. Everything from houses for them to our education wonder just what it will be like?

Wish I could have been there Christmas. You sound as if everything was pretty nice. I was glad to get your letter so close to the other one. I think letters written more often, although maybe not as long are really best. A person doesn't really know just what a letter can mean. It may not even contain anything of interest, but just the feel that it was a letter means a great deal, especially if that letter is from someone whom the person thinks a great deal of.

Well I've began to ramble and you'll be tired of reading this mess. Perhaps I can write a better one next time. Probably I won't sleep all day and will be able to think. So until next I'll keep watching the mail for a letter from you and as ever.

Love,
Frank

While in Columbia, she taught at a nearby rural school to augment my father's small scholarship and GI Bill payments.

One day Dad called and asked her to meet him at the pathology department so she could read to him while he worked...she fainted while he was cutting into one of the cadavers. After that she drew some lines around what she would help with.

Mom's stories about those first years of marriage were filled with love. They had little money and every cent was focused on the goal of Dad becoming a doctor. Instead of despair over their lack of material items, they laughed together.

One of her favorite stories was about the time Dad gave her a gift for a birthday or an anniversary or maybe "just because." It was a very inexpensive bauble, but it was lovingly gift wrapped. When she opened it, tucked under the gift so that it could not be missed, was a price tag of $25.00. That would have been an exorbitant sum for them and much greater than the gift could possibly have cost. Dad acted surprised when he saw the tag and said "Oh, I meant to remove that."

In 1947, the University of Missouri did not have a four-year medical school, so my father transferred to the University of Tennessee, in Memphis, to finish his education. Until my father left for the service, neither of them had lived outside of their insular Southwest Missouri farming community. This was a real city, and a segregated southern city. For a short time my mother worked at a big city department store and she told the story of being reprimanded by her boss when she called a "colored" woman "Ma'am."

My older sister, Lou Ann, was born in Memphis. Although she does not remember it, she attended my father's graduation from medical school. Dad spent a year as an intern at Baptist Memorial

Hospital in Memphis. When I was working at the Federal Deposit Insurance Corporation in the 1990's, I made several business trips to Memphis. I was in meetings most of the days and did not have time for sightseeing—by the time I got to Graceland, the gates were closed. However, I did drive past Baptist Memorial Hospital, a much more important landmark for me. It was the highlight of my trip.

BAPTIST MEMORIAL HOSPITAL
899 MADISON AVENUE
MEMPHIS 3, TENNESSEE

FRANK S. GRONER, ADMINISTRATOR

August 9, 1951

Dr. Isaac F. Sweaney
Missouri Methodist Hospital
St. Joseph, Missouri

Dear Dr. Sweaney:

We are in the process of sending intern evaluations to the deans of various medical schools, and I am pleased to report to you that you ranked very high.

It is not our custom to advise interns of their rank, but because of a notation which was made on a number of your evaluations, I am sending this note to you to express my appreciation of your fine work as an intern.

Incidentally, of the thirty men evaluated, you ranked first in chart work.

With assurance of my best wishes for your success, I am

Very truly yours,

Frank S. Groner
Administrator

FSG:rm

I found this letter folded behind the picture of Dad that was always displayed prominently in our house.

Holt County Sentinel June 22, 1952

In 1951, Dad was looking for a surgical residency program. He had been successful in Tennessee, gaining recognition for his work as an intern, but he wanted to return to his home state. Missouri Methodist Hospital in St. Joseph, Missouri, had an opening. My parents returned to Missouri, but not to the Ozarks. Unlike the rocky hills of the Ozark mountain region, the Northwest corner of Missouri was prospering from its fertile farm land. It was only a year later that my father learned that Dr. Kearney, from the small near-by town of Oregon in Holt County, was retiring and was interested in selling his practice.

HOLT COUNTY, 1952

How All Has Been Changed
By The Hand Of Progress!

What wonderful changes a few years have wrought in Northwest Missouri! Less than forty-five years ago not a single white man dwelt within the present limits of Holt and Atchison Counties...their beautiful rolling prairies, their charming timber-fringed streams and enchanting groves were the home of the antelope, the elk, the buffalo and the red man. How all has been changed by the hand of progress!

— The History of Holt and Atchison Counties, Missouri, 1882

Holt County is small, nestled on the edge of the Missouri River bluffs. It stretches about twenty five miles wide and its southern edge is about thirty miles north of St. Joseph. The Iowa border is approximately sixty miles north of the southern county line and depending on where you cross the river on the west, you will land either in Kansas or Nebraska. The farm land is fertile, and a source of pride to residents who claimed in the 1950s that "the Missouri River bottom land between Forest City and Omaha is some of the richest farmland in the world." They may have been right.

By the twentieth century, the county was an established, prosperous community. Scots-Irish and German immigrants had moved into the area in the 1840s. The rich hill land was quickly settled and western migration moved onward. The families that stayed in northern Missouri put down deep roots. They passed their land onto their sons, who married the daughters of neighboring families. Family names such as Kurtz, Markt, Banks, and Kunkel still make up a large portion of the small telephone directory. These hard-working farmers exhibited more than a little of the traditional American Protestant Work ethic.

Small towns are not all alike, even those within one county. Each community reflects the background of its citizens, and in Holt County, its proximity to the Missouri River. Oregon (population 800) was a somewhat conservative farming community, usually a Republican voting bloc in elections. Mound City, a larger town to the north (population approximately 2,000) more in the center of the county, seemed a little more progressive.

There were people in the county who thought Mound City should be the county seat. It would have made sense. It was larger and more centrally located. County history records several fights to move the Courthouse to Mound City but the governmental center remained in Oregon. Other small Holt County towns such as Forest City, Craig, and Maitland existed with an independent municipal structure. Further north, away from the influence of St. Joseph and even Kansas City, the economy of the towns seemed to strengthen. In neighboring Atchison County, Tarkio and Rock Port thrived.

Life in these small communities revolved around the schools. The natural rivalry between the towns was played out on football fields and basketball courts. Highway 59 combined with Highway 275 as it curved north toward the Iowa line. The 275 Conference governed high school sports. Each school's mascot was well-identified with the community: the Oregon Pirates played the Forest City Bobcats and the Mound City Panthers. The games were hotly contested, replayed endlessly in discussions at local gatherings, in restaurants, barber shops, and drinking establishments. The triumphs and tragedies of the games were always the featured stories in the Holt County Sentinel (Oregon's paper) and the Mound City News Independent.

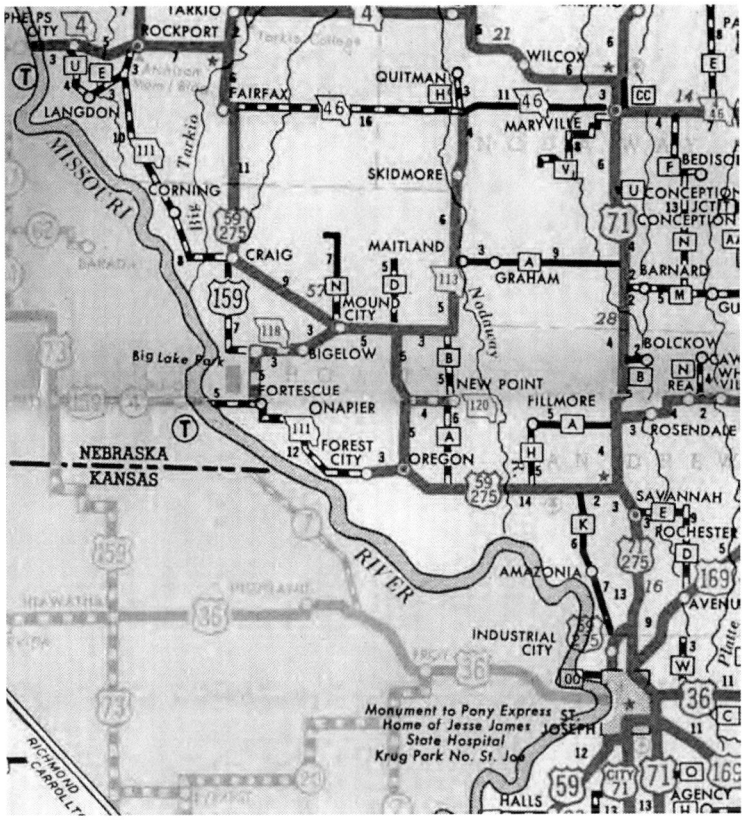

1950 Missouri State Highway Commission Map of Northwest Missouri

Oregon was a pretty town in 1952. It was designed around a square with the courthouse, a beautiful building erected in 1881, at its center. The commercial establishments were built on the streets surrounding the governmental offices. All commerce revolved around the farm economy, and the grocery, hardware and farming supply stores reflected the needs of the community.

Holt County Courthouse
The Courthouse built in 1881 was described
in an early county history as comparing
"in external appearance with the best in the land."
It was destroyed by fire in 1965.

The community was patriotic. Just a few years earlier, Holt County had sent boys to Europe and the Pacific. Myron Noellsch flew planes over Europe, dropping paratroopers involved in the Market Garden Campaign. He returned to Oregon a war hero, married one of the local town beauties, and settled into farming on his family farm. When the Japanese attacked Pearl Harbor, Dean Kreek was on the battleship Nevada playing a trumpet in the band.

Boys may have gone to Korea in the early 1950s, but the county still held World War II in its collective memory. The Veterans of Foreign Wars and the American Legion openly competed for membership. In November of 1952, the county overwhelmingly voted to put the war hero, Ike, in the White House by a margin of 3,476 votes for Eisenhower to 1,487 votes for Stevenson.

Oregon, like many small communities, did not immediately embrace outsiders. It could occasionally surprise, however. The town may have been shocked in 1954 when Nick Ferguson, after spending time in occupied Japan, returned to Missouri with a Japanese wife, Mrs. Sumiko Ferguson. But even with World War II still fresh in many minds, I never heard any negative talk in the town about Nick's choice. I do know his family welcomed his new wife into their lives.

Maybe it was because Sumi clearly wanted to be part of America that the town accepted her. When she began to study for her citizenship exams, Dad told Nick to tell her to call Iris. Mom tutored her in American history and civics. Dad once said that Sumi quickly embraced the culture of her adopted land; she definitely no longer walked two steps behind her husband! But she did not leave all of her culture behind. I remember being invited to the Ferguson's home one night for an authentic Japanese dinner. When a beaten raw egg was passed, Dad just looked at it, passed it on, and said "I already had mine today." Teasing as always. That was his style. (Dad was also known for being a little sensitive about eggs. He always insisted that Mom serve fresh apricots cut side up so that they would not look like the yolks of raw eggs.)

As Sumi became more Americanized, she not only adopted American values but even her children began to look more American. It was almost as if Sumi's genes changed the longer she lived in her adopted country.

In his heart, Nick was a mountain man. It is very easy to picture him as a fur trapper in the early 1800s. He preferred the woods—hunting, fishing and camping—to town. He and Sumi ultimately left Oregon to live in the wilderness of Montana.

Oregon also accepted the Sweaney family. We were clearly identified as "Oregon People." Dad became part of the fabric of the community.

His patients were his friends and neighbors. He saw them on the street, visited with them in the stores, and joked with them at local events.

Dad's influence, however, extended beyond our little town. He treated patients in all the small towns, knew the country roads that linked them together, and was welcomed in farm houses throughout Holt County and into neighboring Atchison and Nodaway Counties. People from Mound City, Craig, and Forest City remember Dad, and if they were born between October 1952 and July of 1960 will likely say, "Doc Sweaney delivered me."

Dad with a friend, Seth Curtis, at Scheib's Hardware.

I Don't Need Any Money.
I'll Put It On
The Sweaney Tab.

— Jim Sweaney, 4 years old

Oregon's economy ran on a "charge and carry" basis in the 1950s. This did not mean that people used charge cards. It would be decades before people in the United States would routinely carry plastic in their wallets. Instead, each merchant had a small tin box by the cash register. In it, arranged in alphabetical order, were cards bearing the name of the town's residents. When we purchased an item, the merchant pulled out our card and added the name of the item and its amount to the running tab. Each month or so, the family breadwinner or his wife was expected to visit the store and pay the accumulated bill.

Mom sent me to the grocery store for small items. Everyone knew I was one of the Sweaney children. When I purchased an item it would automatically be added to my family's bill. Once I went to Scheib's Hardware by myself to buy a present for my McCluey grandparents. I very proudly bought them a toaster and charged it to our family's account. Mom had to accompany me to the store the next day. They could not use the toaster because their Ozark farm did not have electricity. We bought them a set of blue and white dishes in its place.

Inside Scheib's Hardware circa 1950. (courtesy of Judy Scheib)

If a bill was large enough to warrant writing a check, the merchant had a set of blank checks for each of the area banks. He would ask which bank the customer used. He would then hand the individual a counter check for that financial institution. The banks were small enough that each account owner could be identified by his or her name, so there was no need for account numbers. The signed check would be processed by a teller at the bank, and the signature would be the only identification required.

Each of the small towns in the county had at least one bank. In Oregon, we had two: the Citizen's Bank and the Zook and Roecker Bank. My family banked at Zook and Roecker, an old Holt County institution. Levi Zook had come to the county in 1842. He later joined with a Civil War veteran, Captain Albert Roecker, to form the Zook and Roecker Bank. Their names indicated the German heritage of many of the people of Holt County.

The banking system for Zook and Roecker was not automated until early in the 1980s. After I moved to Washington, D.C. in 1974, my mother sent me a check for $20.00. When I took it to my bank to deposit it, the teller looked at it and said they could not process it; it did not have an account number. I tried to explain to the young woman that in Oregon you did not need account numbers—everyone in town knew my mother, and probably knew how much money she had in the bank! She looked at me totally confused and said, "Every bank account has to have a number." The D.C. bank had to place a phone call to Zook and Roecker before they would even consider processing the check.

North side of the town square, Oregon, Missouri circa 1950 (courtesy of Judy Scheib)

On the north side of the square was the post office, Bill Rich's drugstore, Worley's Dry Goods, Citizen's Bank, two grocery stores (Evans and Kreeks), and several other businesses including a tavern that sat at the end of the street. The commercial establishments extended to the west to include the Zook and Roecker Bank, the telephone office, and a movie theatre. The tavern owner, Mr. Branson, and his family were the source of much town gossip. It was said that his daughters were "Playboy Bunnies," although I am not sure if their careers rose to that level of distinction.

On the west side of the square were another grocery store, Hy-Klas, the Richards Law Office, the library, and the most important store of my youth, Scheib's Hardware. Scheib's sold everything that was important to me: the tea set from Dad, pretty china teacups from my mother at Christmas and birthdays, glass figurines that little girls love, dolls and bikes.

I understand that for adults they also sold traditional hardware items.

The picture below of the west side of the town square was taken shortly before the Richard's Law office and the town library were

The law office and the town library replaced the third building from the left.
(courtesy of the Richard's family)

built, and before my parents moved to town. The law office and the town library took over the building with the "Philco" sign, and my dad's office was located at the end of this street on the southwest corner of the square, although it is not in the picture.

Advertisment for Worley's Holt County Sentinel, June 20, 1952.

Worley Mercantile sold dry goods. These included material, buttons, and thread. This advertisement shows Worley's carried groceries but in my memory selling groceries was the province of three other stores on the square: Kreeks, Evans, and Hy-Klas.

Golden Crust Bread, H-OZ. LOAVES	2 for 25c
Angel Food Cake, large size .	45c
Layer Cakes- white, devils food	45c
Do Nuts, glazed doz. . . .	39c
Fruit Cocktail, HyKlas 2½ size	39c
Apple Butter, HyKlas 2 lb. jar	20c
Peanut Butter, Hyklas 2 lb. jar	65c
Posttoasties, large size . . .	27c
Ground Beef, our own lb. . .	49c
Fryers, 2½ to 2¾ lbs. dressed	1.25

APRICOTS, CELERY, CARROTS, APPLES, TOMATOES, LEMONS, ORANGES, POTATOES, GRAPEFRUIT, BANANAS
FROZEN FOODS—ICE CREAM

Hy-Klas FOOD STORES

No. 42   Good Things to Eat   WE RESERVE THE RIGHT TO LIMIT QUANTITIES   OREGON, Mo

FREE DELIVERY AT 10 O'CLOCK EACH THURSDAY

Advertised grocery prices the week of June 20, 1952.

In Worley's basement, down the steps in the center of the store, were the shoes. Each year before school started, we would visit Worley's to buy tennis and saddle shoes. Tennis shoes were always white and could be cleaned in the washing machine, dried in the clothes drier, and then whitened with shoe polish. Saddle shoes were called that because of the decorative panel in brown or black placed at mid foot.

Mary El Buck helped her parents run the store. The Bucks were big sports fans and everyone in town knew that the most recent Oregon high school sports event would be replayed endlessly in discussions at Worley's.

The Oregon Theatre was showing the Van Heflin-Patricia Neal movie, "Week End with Father", the week my parents moved to Oregon. Mound City's State Theatre also showed movies, so if we did not like the ones showing in Oregon, or had already seen them, Mound City's State Theatre provided another option for a Saturday night movie. During the fifties, Mound City also had a drive-in theatre right outside of town.

OREGON THEATRE

Sunday and Monday, June 22-23:
Van Heflin, Patricia Neal
"WEEK END WITH FATHER"
News   Cartoon

Wednesday and Thursday, June 25-26:
Ava Gardner, James Mason in
"PANDORA AND THE FLYING DUTCHMAN"
TECHNICOLOR
Cartoon

Friday and Saturday, June 27-28:
Jeff Chandler, Beverly Tyler
"THE BATTLE OF THE APACHE"
TECHNICOLOR
PLUS: "IT HAPPENED ALL NIGHT"

The Oregon Theater was playing "Week End With Father" when my parents arrived.

Movies about the potential danger of technology were very popular in the 1950s. In them, scientific advances resulted in new monsters and sometimes a revival of old ones. I had trouble sleeping after seeing a movie in the Oregon Theatre that featured stop motion footage of dinosaurs and giant lizards.

A River With A Personality

There is only one river with a personality, a sense of humor, and a woman's caprice; a river that goes traveling sidewise, that interferes in politics, rearranges geography, and dabbles in real estate; a river that plays hide and seek with you today and tomorrow follows you around like a pet dog with a dynamite cracker tied to his tail. That river is the Missouri.

— George Fitch, 1907

In 2011, floods devastated the Missouri River floodplain. In October, my husband's cousin was to be married in Omaha. We decided to attend the wedding and to combine the trip with a quick pilgrimage to Holt County. I had followed the news reports of the devastating floods that had for months closed I-29. Fortunately, it reopened the week we arrived in Omaha. As we drove down the interstate into Missouri, tears came to my eyes. The land looked like a war zone. Big Lake State Park and Camp Rulo, places that played such significant roles in my childhood, were gone.

Holt County has long been defined by the muddy Missouri River. It not only defines the county's western boundary but also much of its history. President Thomas Jefferson in 1804 directed Meriwether Lewis and William Clark to explore the Missouri River. Holt County residents are very proud that this expedition camped in the county and local historians claim that they can identify the spot where Lewis and Clark tied their boats. William Clark wrote about the scenery as the expedition moved up the Missouri River from present-day Kansas City as "one of the most butifull [sic] Plains I ever saw."

Forest City, population fewer than 300, lies three miles to the west of Oregon. In the first part of the nineteenth century, Forest City was a prosperous, booming river port situated almost equidistant between Kansas City and Omaha. The Missouri River begins in North Dakota and flows south forming the border between several Midwestern states. As it approaches the midpoint of Missouri, it divides the state in half as it journeys east to Saint Louis where it empties into the Mississippi. In the 1800s, Forest City was strategically located on a bend on the river and was uniquely positioned to prosper from the economic boom that followed the Civil War. In her book, *150 Years of Forest City, Missouri History* (2007), Peggy Ann Bush Edwards notes that in 1868 merchants shipped 150,000 bushels of grain and over 50,000 fat hogs from this bustling market center. The future looked bright for this growing city.

The Missouri River, however, had a mind of its own and decided to re-write the future. In the summer of 1868, the river flooded. The economic fortunes of Forest City would be forever changed that summer. "On the never-to-be-forgotten morning" of August 10, 1868, Forest City residents awoke to find that the main channel of the river was now flowing two and one-half miles to the west leaving the town inland and robbing Forest City of both its commercial promise and its prestige.

My parents arrived in Holt County in the summer of 1952 on the heels of another epic Missouri River flood. Land would be underwater for months, and it would take the devastation wrought by the flood of 2011 before "old timers" would concede 1952's title as the "flood of all floods." Until the summer of 2011, when Northwest Missourians talked about the changeable Missouri River they would start with tales of the spring of 1952.

As is the cause of most of the floods on the Missouri River, it was weather in the Dakotas that created the conditions for the great flood of 1952. In the north, winter had been especially long with heavy and frequent snowfalls. In March, the upper Midwest experienced warm temperatures causing the snow to melt more quickly than normal. The mighty Missouri River did not need any more encouragement than this influx of water to follow its inclination to leave its banks.

"On the northern plains in late March lay the entire accumulation of winter snow and ice. It contained all the potentials for destructive spring floods. It needed only a sudden period of thawing high temperatures to transform the snow into flood water.

The month of March 1952 added the final stage setting for the greatest flood the upper Missouri River has ever visited upon the people of the valley since the white man settled here."

Brig Gen. D. G. Shingler, Missouri River Division engineer with the Army Corps of Engineers, said in a speech on April 23, 1952.

On Easter Sunday 1952, when the Christian community of Holt County looked to God (and that would have been the entire county), the term "risen" did not just apply to their Savior but also to the Missouri River. In southern Holt County, "the flood was six feet deep in many houses and left mud on everything. Cleaning the homes was a major task, and those involved were given free typhoid shots."

Missouri River spread over fields in Holt County, spring of 1952.

As the water receded, a trusting public put its faith in the assurances that the damage on the scale of 1952 could be avoided. Local levy districts joined the Federal Government in creating an intricate system, giving citizens the false assurance that man could control and tame the muddy river.

President Turmen returning to the Midwest to view the 1952 Flood Damage. (courtesy of the Douglas County Historical Society)

The engineers channeled the river to follow a new path, moving the river to the east. When the water subsided, new, rich, fertile land was left. Farmers reclaimed the Missouri River bottom planting corn on new acres. Land that once had been on the eastern side of the river was now on the west. Since the border between Missouri and Kansas was based on the river, state lines were redrawn. Land once in Missouri was on the other side of the river and now claimed by Kansas. Legal battles over taxation rights lasted for decades. Eventually the court determined that the river was once again the legal boundary between the two states and Kansas held the taxing rights to the rich bottom land.

Floods in 1993 and then in 2011 would prove that the river had an independent spirit, and the Corps would be unable to keep its earlier promises. History is left to be written regarding the aftermath of the flood of 2011. Environmentalists talk of returning the river to the "days of Lewis and Clark." The Corps of Engineers seem to be giving up on their ability to control the river by levies. Although historic lessons might lead one to believe otherwise, contemporary engineers harbor the belief that they can control the path of the independent river by making strategic decisions in the Dakotas.

HEALTH CARE
(FIFTIES STYLE)

KID, THAT FIRST DAY DOC WAS BUSY, BUSY; YOU MIGHT SAY SWAMPED.

— Bette Williams, 2012

Holt County was still recovering from the floods when my parents arrived on July 1, 1952. Several people had already met my dad. Bette Williams remembers the young doctor who stopped by the hospital in St. Joseph to see her after her son Ed was born. He had noticed on her chart that she was from Oregon. He said he did not know if he would have any patients but he was looking forward to moving to the town. But Bette remembers Dad was busy from the start. (Bette starts all sentences with 'Kid'.)

He hung out his shingle at an office prominently located in the heart of the town across from the courthouse.

Dad's shingle is now on display in a glass case in the Holt County Courthouse.

I still see the office with a little girl's eyes. I was very surprised when I recently visited the building that it was so incredibly small. Now it is a beauty shop, but as I walked through it, I remembered it as it was fifty-plus years earlier.

Dad's Office building still sits on the square in Oregon, but now it is a beauty shop.

There was of course the waiting room. There still are several pictures of me as a child in that room. My dad's office and principle examining room was on the right as you entered the building. Above his desk were pictures of the many children that he delivered.

Behind this room was a lab, and to the left a hallway that led to a bathroom and another examining room. This room held an X-ray machine. I can remember playing on this expensive piece of equipment when I was a child. This memory does give credence to the view of many people in town that we kids had way too much freedom around that office.

When I close my eyes, I can see the refrigerator that stood by the hallway. It always contained bottles of Pepsi. Dad would stop by it as he quickly moved between the two examining rooms to see the patients that seemed to always be waiting.

He would drink half of the bottle going and the other half on his return. I know that he used the sugar and caffeine to give him energy to stifle his exhaustion, but it was a habit that also fed his obesity.

The number of people who came through that small office is staggering. Only one set of official records from my dad's practice still exists. In 1989 after my mother's death, we kids spent an afternoon burning any remaining medical records. Although some of these were created thirty-seven years earlier, we were still very aware that they could contain secrets, and in a small town, thirty-seven years is not a long time. If any secrets were to be revealed, they would still be very damaging to reputations and social standing.

I did decide to keep one of the large volumes labeled, *The Physician's Daily Record*. It was the volume recording my father's first full year of practice, 1953. Entered by hand were the names of the patients seen and the money collected for the visit. Turning to the entries for the last month of the year, you can begin to get a feel for his life.

Christmas that year was on a Friday. On Thursday, Christmas Eve, he saw sixty-six patients in his office. On the following day, Christmas, he saw twelve people. On December 26, Saturday, people who had not come the previous two days flooded the office, and he saw 103 people. The holiday weekend was not over. On Sunday, December 27, Dad opened his office door to twenty-eight people. In many ways, that was a very typical week for that year. His office staff recorded that he saw 14,766 patients in that year, *not including* house calls and hospital visits.

The *Physician's Daily Record* also proves another piece of family lore. There were many entries that showed either the notation "no charge" or that indicated that no money was collected. There are no entries indicating that insurance payments were a factor in 1953. The record indicates that $28,896.18 was collected for the year. If you do the math, that works out to slightly less than $2.00 per patient. That was his first year. His life and practice became

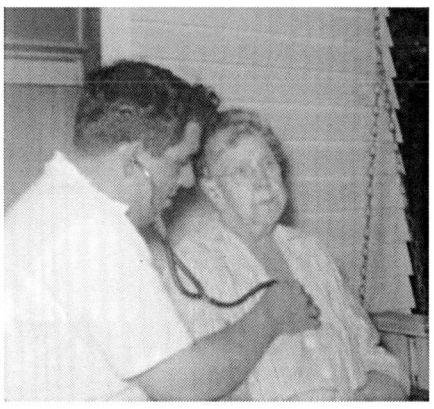

Sitting on a porch swing is a good way to get a relaxed reading on a heartbeat.

increasingly busier and more intense. It would be very interesting to know the numbers from his last full year of practice.

Dad just knew how to make his patients feel comfortable.

Fifty-two years later, people still remember their visits to Dad. They do not recall being rushed through an assembly line. He knew them and he knew their families. An individual's status in the society of Northwest Missouri was not a factor. He paid attention to each person and listened to his or her concerns and ailments. He served lawyers, shopkeepers, and farmers, rural and town people. They remember his wit and most of all his care.

No One Ever Called Her "Anna."

— Mom remembering Mrs. Narans

Dad's first act in establishing his life as a country doctor was to hire Mrs. Anna Narans as his nurse, administrator, and general manager. It was a very wise decision. Mrs. Narans was an important mainstay of the Oregon community. She was an established Oregon personality and helped Dad carve out his role in the tight-knit community. She was already recognized for her generous spirit. Previously, she had opened her home to an orphaned teenager, Russell Williams, so that he could continue his high school education.

Oregon was a first-name community. I called all adults by their first names. But, no one ever called Mrs. Narans, "Anna." Even my mother called her by her formal name. To Dad, she was Mama Narans. Mrs. Narans daughter, Phyllis, was a nurse who sometimes assisted in

Mrs. Narans. School children always wanted Mrs. Narans to administer their shots. Dad did not have her touch!

the office. What strong, committed, women they were! There was nothing mild-mannered or meek about those two women.

—Louie's

Phyllis Narans

Leonard Narans, her son, was in Oregon when Dad was getting the office in order. He told Dad, "You really made a good choice in mother. She can also mend your clothes, cut your hair, fix small appliances and if you push her far enough, she can really preach a good sermon."

The last was never necessary, but Dad did tell Mrs. Narans, "If you want to bring up your sewing machine it would be okay because we will not be busy at first."

Phyllis said, "That was 'famous last words' as they were busy from the start." Every once in a while Doc would say to her mother, "In what corner are you going to put your sewing machine?"

Yvonne Lippold was a recent high school graduate when she began working as my dad's receptionist. She was a little gullible and Dad loved to tease her. On her first day of work, Dad brought out a set of tools. He seemed quite upset and told her he could not get the tools to work. He directed her to take them back to Muriel Wardlow at Scheib's Hardware. He wanted a refund. Yvonne, very dutifully, wanting to please her new boss, took the tools to Muriel. She told him very seriously, "Doc wants his money back." Muriel just started laughing. He had loaned the tools to Dad.

Maxine Edwards, Mary Kreek, and Pearl Moore rounded out the staff. Pearl cleaned the office during the early morning hours. She was credited with keeping a man alive with 1958 style CPR until Dad, called out of a short sleep, returned to the office. Yvonne became a stay-at-home-mom after her daughter was born, and Pat Kee became Dad's receptionist.

These people were all players on my childhood stage. Our lives were intertwined; it is the way of a small town. Yvonne and Pat's families went to our church. Pat's mother was my advisor in Rainbow Girls, and later Pat's brother coached my brother's football team. Lou Ann was a flower girl in Yvonne and Paul Markt's wedding. My younger sister Carry worked for Paul when she was in high school. They remember me as a little girl, usually in Lou Ann's shadow, with bows stuck on my head with scotch tape because barrettes fell out of my baby-fine hair.

I Remember Your Home. It Was Where We Went If We Were Sick And Your Dad's Office Was Closed.

— Steve Burrier, my classmate, 2012

In July of 1952, while my dad was busy setting up his office on the southwest corner of the town square, my mother was setting up house in the upstairs rooms of a big house on the edge of town. It was built in the first decade of the 20th century, a large two-story white clapboard set on a big corner lot. The house had many of the architectural features that were popular at the time that it was built: two porches, interesting bay windows in the downstairs rooms, very high ceilings, and crown molding.

The two rooms downstairs were separated by a heavy sliding door. My dad set up an auxiliary office area in one of those rooms to see patients. They soon would be coming to the house at all hours when, of course, his office was officially closed.

My mother was almost eight months pregnant with me, and had a very active little daughter, my three year old sister Lou Ann. It must have been hard for my mother to move to a new community during a very difficult pregnancy in the heat of a Missouri summer. I was born, prematurely, a week after they moved in, on July 8.

Mom and Dad arrived in Oregon with absolutely no financial resources. After my difficult birth, Dad hired a teen-ager, Evelyn Matthews, to help Mom. That summer they canned tomatoes from a bushel that had been left by the door to pay for a medical bill. The teenager was amazed at how poor the new family seemed. Evelyn accompanied Mom to the Ozarks to see both sets of my grandparents. She was not prepared for the poverty she saw in those foothills and thought, "How did he ever go to medical school?"

Lou Ann shortly after moving to Oregon in 1952

My parents initially rented the upstairs rooms of the big house but a short time later they bought the house. By 1952, it had already begun to show its age. In recent years, it has become very popular to restore old houses. I have thought that our old house would have been a really great candidate for restoration. But, my parents were much too busy and did not have the finances or the abilities to be home restorers. The house never lived up to its potential, and has since been torn down.

Dr. Calkin was the D.O. (Doctor of Osteopathic Medicine) in town. Dad held him in warm regard and did not feel that they were competing for business. The Calkin's house was much nicer and newer than ours. It was a fact that anyone could recognize. My dad used to drive visitors around Oregon and point out the Calkin's home by saying, "There's my competitor's shack."

I Can Make A Living Delivering Kurtz Babies.

— Dad, 1952

As soon as Dr. Sweaney hung out his shingle patients began to arrive. First, he attracted patients without established relationships with doctors in St. Joseph. It was a long trek to St. Joe and very difficult for many of the poorer, rural people to make the drive; in the fifties the drive took over an hour on the rough, curved, roads. Later, the interstate highway system would shorten this trip, cutting the drive time in half. But many of the more established families took a "wait and see" attitude to the new doctor. After all, he was a newcomer. That fall, however, with the birth of a Kurtz baby girl the town truly embraced his medical practice.

In October, Jim Fitzgerald, a local county official, called Dad. His daughter, Darlyne Kurtz, had gone into premature labor at her home. There was not going to be time to take her to St. Joe, and besides her doctor was on a hunting trip. Dad went to Ed and Darlyne's house and delivered Gail in one of their bedrooms. She was the first Kurtz girl after a long line of boys. He came home that night and told Mom that he thought he could have a place in this community, and he joked that he could make a living just delivering Kurtz babies. By the end the decade, he was delivering most of the babies born during the baby-boom years in Holt County.

Holt County Kurtzes

When I think of rock-solid Midwestern family farmers, I think of Kurtzes.

The history of Southern Holt County would have been different if Mrs. Isaac Kurtz had born girls instead of boys. In 1857, two years after arriving in America from Germany, Isaac Kurtz and Mary Seaman married and settled in Holt County. They were blessed by eleven sons and two daughters. This pattern of many sons and few daughters would hold true for future Kurtz families. Throughout the generations, the sons stayed to farm the land.

I remember a story about a young man who had met a pretty Oregon girl at an end-of-the-year party at Northwest Missouri State in Maryville. He had not obtained her phone number but wanted to continue the relationship. By that time, they had gone separate ways for summer vacation. He thought, "How difficult could it be to track her down? After all, Oregon is so small. How many Kurtzes could there be in the phone directory?" The directory assistance operator just laughed when he tried to reach her without knowing her father's name.

On a recent visit with Gary Kurtz, a fourth generation Holt County Kurtz, I asked him, jokingly, if there was an abnormality in his genes. *How, as a Kurtz, had he fathered three daughters and no sons?*

YOU COULD SET YOUR CLOCK
BY DOC SWEANEY.

— Jim Kurtz, 2012

FAIRFAX COMMUNITY HOSPITAL

Most of the babies were not born at home. They were delivered at the small Community Hospital in Fairfax. The original facility built in 1949 had plans for thirty-two beds, but one four-person room had six beds in it to make it a thirty-four bed hospital. In 1952, a second floor waiting room was converted to a three-person room, increasing the total to thirty-seven beds.

Each morning, seven days a week, Dad would begin his day by driving thirty-five minutes to Fairfax; forty miles away from our home in Oregon. I am told by farmers living along old Route 59 that they would watch him speeding pass their land the same time each morning, judging their own schedules by his, and checking their watches to make sure that their time pieces were

Fairfax Forum - July 17, 1952.

ANOTHER PHYSICIAN JOINS FAIRFAX HOSPITAL STAFF

Frank Sweaney, M. D., who recently located at Oregon for the practice of his profession, has joined the medical staff of the Fairfax Community hospital.

accurate. As he drove through Mound City, he would slow down a little to make sure that the telephone operator was not waving him down to alert him to an emergency.

The hospital was only three years old when Dad moved to the area. He joined a small group of doctors who practiced in the small communities north of Oregon in neighboring Atchison County. These doctors, among them Dr. Niedermeyer of Tarkio and Dr. Carpenter of Rock Port, lived much closer to the hospital and to each other than Dad did. They developed a cohesive, collegial relationship. Dad's practice soon became the largest, covered the most distance, and resulted in the largest number of patients in the hospital at any given point in time.

Northwest Missourians had a personal relationship with Fairfax Community Hospital. It was their hospital. The hospital created a brochure in honor of its fifth anniversary in 1954. My father is listed as Vice-President of the Staff. The brochure states, "As much a part of the modern community as the church and school, the hospital has been accepted by the community as part of its responsibility." This warm feeling about hospitals seems to have been prevalent during the 1950s. In the 1954 television series *Janet Dean: Registered Nurse,* actress Ella Raines tells a young Sal Mineo, an emergency room patient (in one of his first acting jobs), "not to worry about paying for his operation, that the hospital would pick up the tab."

DOC SWEANEY WAS A COUNTRY DOCTOR, BUT HE DID NOT HAVE A HORSE AND BUGGY. DOC SWEANEY HAD AN OLDSMOBILE.

—Paul Markt, 2012

Before Dad moved up to Oldsmobiles, my parents owned a 1955 Chevy. While it was still quite new, Dad put a significant scratch on it, but he didn't immediately tell my mom about the damage. When Mom drove it the next day, she noticed the scratch, assumed that she had caused the damage and felt terrible. Never

I am standing with Lou Ann next to 1955 Chevy outside Dad's office.

one to miss a chance to tease my mother, Dad let her think that she had caused the scratch. But he never could keep a joke to himself for very long. Several days later, Mom and the whole town knew about the scratch and who had really caused it. People in town still repeat the story of Doc's joke on Iris.

When Lowell Ripley, of Crouse Motors in Mound City, read that the new Old's 98 came with a steering wheel that tilted, he knew that was the car for Dad. By then, my dad's weight issues were noticeable. Dad's new car was stylish, black, and also served as the town's ambulance.

One day Dad returned to Crouse Motors with a complaint: he could no longer move the driver's seat. Lowell found the mechanism blocked by a stiff, round ice cream carton. Inside of the carton was a pint of whiskey given to Dad by a farmer to pay for a house call. He had forgotten about placing it under the seat probably to hide it from Mom who did not approve of spirits. In contrast, farm wives made a point of giving Dad samples of their home cooking, showing appreciation and love for him with the gift of food. To quote one of Dad's friends, "Doc ate his way around the county during those house calls."

As Dad drove out of town, he would stop at Bill Rayhill's station to fill his car with the twenty-to-thirty-cents-a-gallon gas. Bill would clean the windshield, check the oil

Original Crouse Brothers Announcement (courtesy Bob Crouse)

and other fluids, and add the service to his tab. After Dad's death, Mom was not able to see Bill immediately to pay the very large tab that had accumulated through Dad's daily stops at the station. When she did pay the bill she apologized for not stopping by earlier. Bill said, "Iris, I never thought about it for a moment." Mom never forgot Bill's graciousness. We never used any other filling station except Bill's.

RAYHILL'S SKELLY SERVICE

GUARANTEED SKELLY PRODUCTS

Oregon, Missouri

Bill Rayhill, Prop.   Telephone 144

Advertisement from the 1954 Fall Festival Brochure.

When asked about Dad, the other doctors all commented on one thing. Doc Sweaney had a driver. Kenneth Jackson drove Dad at night allowing him to sleep between house calls. In my memory, Kenneth Jackson was simply another "good ole boy" from Missouri. I was very surprised to learn this year that he was a University of Missouri graduate. They must have really enjoyed each other's company and shared interesting conversations while driving along those dark, lonely, country roads.

IF I HADN'T GONE ON HOUSE CALLS, I MIGHT NEVER HAVE SEEN HIM.

— Mom, 1982

Our family life revolved around Dad's practice. His office and car were where our family gathered. More often than not, his long day was followed by house calls. Even after his staff left for the day, Dad still saw patients, sometimes as late as 10:00 p.m. Mom often brought us to the office in the evening, keeping an eye on us as she acted as his receptionist, directing patients, and answering the phone.

Left: Mom answering the phone in Dad's office.

Right: Mom, Lou Ann, and I in Dad's office, 1953.

Family meals were a rarity during those years. We often ate at a little restaurant in nearby Forest City called the Green Kitchen owned by Sandy and Jannett Dobbins. People knew that if they needed my father he might be found at the Green Kitchen.

Jannett Dobbins, overlooking a dinner being prepared in the Green Kitchen. In the 1953 Fall Festival brochure, the Green Kitchen was advertised as "A Good Place to Eat." So true, so true.

I recall Dad receiving an emergency call at the Green Kitchen. He promptly left the table and drove the family car to the caller's house. Sheriff Ramsey had to drive us home. I was told by one farmer that he could picture Dad sitting down to eat at the Green Kitchen during the last year of his life, so exhausted that he fell asleep over his food.

Ah, but what food. Jannett spent much of her time in the kitchen, peeling potatoes, cutting them into thin strips, and deep frying them into golden and delicious French fries. The Green Kitchen has long since closed but a recent meal at Forest City Diner (the Twins Café of my youth) of a cheeseburger and homemade French fries—a sinful treat—brought back the memories. I don't think I have ever tasted anything so good.

On Sunday afternoons, we would be loaded into the car so Dad could visit people in their homes. At each stop, the kids would stay in the car playing games with Mom while Dad visited the sick person. We often went to Camp Rulo on the Missouri River in Nebraska for a quick dinner between the calls. Because time was always in short supply, my mother called before we left home to place an order. Camp Rulo was famous for its Missouri River catfish, and Mom ordered catfish dinners for her and Dad. We kids were considered too young to pick out the bones in the fish, so Mom ordered us "catfish chicken." Nebraska had laws that forbade children from being in the bar area so dining rooms had a separate family entrance, but my dad very much enjoyed parading his family through the bar, holding Carry in his arms, to enter the dining room.

When I describe these times, I become aware that they seem, and I think were, more than a little intense. (In today's terminology, you might be tempted to say a "little insane"). Years later, as an adult, I asked my mother about this life. She said, in her matter of fact manner, that if she hadn't gone with him on calls she might never have seen him.

CAMP RULO
Rulo, Nebr.
On the Banks of the Missouri
FISH, CHICKEN and
STEAK DINNERS
Beer, Wines and Liquors
Telephone 301

Advertisement from the 1954 Fall Festival Brochure.

Dad's Olds was well-recognized in the area so the state police did not usually stop him as he sped around the county. Once, however, a young patrolman, distinctive in the western-style hat of the Missouri State Highway Patrol, stopped our car. It might have been on a Sunday afternoon. The whole family was in the car. The patrolman walked away after sheepishly apologizing to my father. My very young brother Jim, he could not have been more than three, said in awe, "Wow, a real cowboy!" It must have been shortly after this stop that Dad obtained a red blinking light that he placed on the top of his car when he needed to speed to an emergency.

Jim during his cowboy phase.

At times, Dad was so busy that Mom had to step in as ambulance driver. Luckily by this time, we had become a two-car family— but only one blinking red light. I recall an instance when my father had already left for the hospital and a local farmer came to the house bleeding from a farm accident. Mom managed to get him into the back seat of her car and drove as fast as she could to Fairfax. Suddenly, behind her, was a State Patrol car with its lights flashing. She stopped the car. The patrolman walked up to the window and seeing Mom and the man in the back seat, said, "I am so sorry, Mrs. Sweaney, I did not recognize your car. Follow me and we will get to the hospital."

My sister, Lou Ann, remembers going on house calls with Dad. In an article written for the Oregon Times Observer in 2005 she recalled:

I remember a flood and we visited a family with several young children. They all had strep throat. We had to get to the house on a raft and I arrived with Dad for the house call with wet shoes and socks. The mother gave me hot cocoa and dry clothing. My mother returned the clothing in the mail. I have no idea who those folks were....

Sometimes, [Dad] road into isolated farms on the county snow plow. I remember watching him go out into a snow covered field alone, to carry a man who had collapsed in the field back to his farm house.

Not all the house calls were in response to a true medical crisis but Dad couldn't know that before he left. Once, parents called him to come to their rural house to treat their small daughter. When Dad arrived, he found that they wanted him to pierce their daughter's ears.

FOUR HOURS, FOUR CALLS, FOUR COUNTIES

— Dr. Jay Milne, 1959

Jay Milne was a medical student at the University of Missouri when he worked one summer at the hospital in Fairfax. He told me the story of going on house calls one night with Dad, and Kenneth Jackson at the wheel. They started from Oregon after Dad's office had closed for the day at 7:00 p.m.

Their first stop was an old farm home in Amazonia. It was only a distance of twenty miles from Oregon but on bumpy country roads, the trip took over thirty-five minutes. The people there were very poor and still used kerosene lamps for light, very unusual for Northern Missouri in the late fifties.

Next was a house in Graham, followed by a visit to a woman in Craig who had a house full of kids and no husband. Finally they checked in on patients at Fairfax around 11:00 p.m. That night they drove at least a hundred miles, a distance repeated on many nights. Dr. Milne, still amazed more than fifty years later, said "Four hours, four calls, four counties."

Doc Sweaney Gave A Pint Of Blood Directly From His Own Body.

— *Peggy Ann Bush Edwards*

Peggy Ann Bush Edwards is a current cultural presence in Southern Holt County, a published author, musician, local historian and civic leader. She shared with me the following story:

In the spring of 1959 or 1960, my grandmother Flossie Bush was ill with a gall bladder that had turned her skin yellow. Her gall bladder was removed at Fairfax Hospital, but for some reason they couldn't stop the bleeding. They used all the Type A positive blood that the hospital had. Her daughter happened to be with her that night and had the same blood type as her mother. They asked if she would donate a pint of blood to her mother. Of course, she said, "Yes." When they were still in need of blood in the emergency situation, Dr. Sweaney (so it was described to me) lay down beside her and gave a pint of blood directly to her from his body thus saving her life.

I think the date was the first year that I was teaching (1959) but it could have been the following year. I was always told that the blood was taken direct from body to body, but not having a medical background I don't know if such a thing is possible.

Ironically, my grandmother outlived Dr. Sweaney.

Anna Lou Doebbeling, a former county official, told me the story of her appendectomy:

Doc Sweaney picked me up at my house and took me to the hospital in Fairfax for my surgery. After surgery, I stayed in the hospital a week to recover. Doc visited me every day. At the end of the week, he took me home, stopping to make house calls along the forty mile route back to Oregon.

It was not only town leaders that my father treated. He had a close relationship with Annie Ben Hayes. At one time the African-American population in Oregon had been large enough to justify a "Colored" church and school, but by the late fifties, ninety-year old Annie Ben Hayes was the only African-American woman left in town. Most of the African-Americans had moved away to work in defense plants during World War II. Lore had it that there were four brothers who married "Annies," so that each Annie took the first name of her husband. Annie Ben had a special relationship to our family. To pay for her medical care, she often cooked us the southern meals that my father loved. Her fried chicken and pepper cold slaw were legendary.

In 2005, Mary Kreek, writing for the *Times Observer*, remembered Annie Ben's frequent calls to Dad's office to talk with him. She would say that she was afraid that this would be her last day on earth and could he come because she believed she was dying. Dad responded by saying, "Oh, I think you will be all right, just you get ready and I'll pick you up when I close the office and take you on house calls with me." She would perk right up, accompany him for several hours, and wouldn't call again for a few weeks.

Annie Ben died in 1961. On her 92nd birthday in 1959, the *Holt County Sentinel* carried an article about her. She told the writer that her "get up and go, seemed to have gone up and went."

This fall when I visited my parents' graves, I stopped for a few minutes by Annie Ben's grave stone to show my respect for this woman who was a fixture in the community during my childhood.

From the Holt County Sentinel 1886

"Miss Annie Jackson (Colored) has just returned from Newton, Ia., where she attended the public school at that place. She was the only colored person in her department and did her race credit with high grades in all branches. She will return to Newton to pass through the higher departments and our only comment is that it is a severe reflection on the Missouri public school system that meritorious persons such as Miss Annie, because of their color, are placed at such a disadvantage in the attainment of an education."

Printed in "Gone Home" by Eileen Deer

THE DOCTORS THERE ARE REALLY ON THE BALL!

— The Singing Doctors, 1958

In 1958, a group of doctors in Springfield in Greene County, Missouri, formed a singing group. The "Singing Doctors" became quite popular and recorded several albums. Their songs were parodies of popular show tunes, full of inside medical humor from the period. My dad brought home one of their first albums. Lou Ann and I listened to these tunes, not understanding many of the lyrics but singing along with them. The musical reprise of the Singing Doctors was "Everything's up-to-date in 'Ole Greene County. The doctors there are really on the ball." The words have stayed with me. Last year when Lou Ann, Carry, and I visited our Sweaney cousins in the Ozarks, we saw the sign for "entering Greene County." Lou Ann and I both said in unison, "Everything's up to date in 'Ole Greene County."

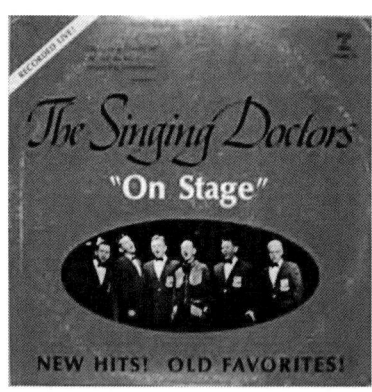

The Singing Doctors "On Stage" album cover (Green County Medical Society.) www.flickr.com/photos/ nichovonakron/394711713/

Consistent with the Sweaney's slightly irreverent sense of

humor was a rousing hootenanny song called "Hemorrhoids." Lou Ann and I sang the chorus loudly around the house:

HEMORRHOIDS

There is much you can say about medicine today
We've made great strides in drugs and surgery
But there's still one disease
That we can't treat with ease
To say you can is perjury!

Chorus:
Hemorrhoids. Often itch and always burn.
Hemorrhoids. Give you that look of concern.
Hemorrhoids. If you think your life is void,
You should have a hemorrhoid!

We use creams and oils and such
But it just don't help us much.
And sitz baths give relief for just awhile.
So we switch to Medicone and a shot of Yellowstone,
But still can't sit and still can't smile

Dad laughed when he heard us singing the chorus. He talked of having us perform the song at his medical association, but my mother did not encourage that idea.

The Singing Doctors' song, "Justified Appendectomy", was to the tune of a romantic song from *My Fair Lady* and it started with the words, "I have often sliced through the skin and more" in place of the lyrics, "I have often walked down this street before." My dad was a general practitioner; as such, he treated all the routine illnesses, but he was also an accomplished surgeon. His residency had been in surgery at Missouri Methodist Hospital in St. Joseph. His name plate proudly read, "I. F. Sweaney, M.D., Physician & Surgeon." (The "I" stands for Isaac, but Dad never used his first name.) He performed appendectomies, tonsillectomies, and removed gallbladders in the small operating rooms at the Community Hospital.

One of his colleagues, Dr. Wallace Carpenter, recalls that my dad's hands were not those of a typical surgeon. They were short and fat, with pudgy fingers. But, he remembers Dad as the "best doctor I ever scrubbed in with" and said that he was one of the best surgeons he ever saw. He told the story of a duel between the two of them over the operating table:

We both had appendectomies scheduled. I told him that I could do mine in twelve minutes. When I finished, I looked at the clock and said, "See, twelve minutes." Your dad had not yet said anything to me, but already taking off his gloves, he responded with that twinkle in his eyes, "Seven minutes."

Dad was active in the Nodaway-Atchison-Gentry-Holt-Worth Counties Medical Society. His involvement with this collegial group must have been important to him. His obituary mentions that he served as its president. I always pictured that with five counties included in the name this group must have been large, full of prestigious doctors.

Recently, I asked Dr. Carpenter about his memories of the society. Dr. Carpenter had been at the University of Missouri Medical School with Dad, went to Illinois when Dad went to the University of Tennessee, but then came to Northwest Missouri and settled in Rock Port at the same time Dad moved to Oregon. He was a little younger than Dad since WWII had interfered with Dad's schooling. Dr. Carpenter, long since retired, laughed when he remembered his group of colleagues from fifty years earlier:

Well, there were probably about eight doctors in our society. We all were practicing in small towns, going on house calls and charging $3.00 for an office visit. None of us liked the St. Joe doctors and the Maryville doctors would have nothing to do with us. Your dad was about treating rural people. There was nothing 'city' about him but he had the largest practice of any of us.

In my house, the term "City Doctor" was said with disdain. It meant a doctor who took Thursday afternoons off to play golf, cared about society more than patients, and saw people only by appointment.

The stories and the songs capture the arrogance and cockiness of professionals who were proud of their skills and were performing work that they enjoyed. In my mind, I picture Dad and Dr. Carpenter as two other surgeons from the 1950s, Hawkeye Pierce and Trapper John McIntire, an image formed from repeated viewings of the hit television show "M*A*S*H" about doctors operating during the Korean War. Dr. Carpenter's words show a professional respect for Dad and a spirit of camaraderie.

However, it is not only the stories that I take away from my conversation with Dr. Carpenter. The two words that he used when he talked about how he was not prepared for my dad's death are what I remember the most: *I grieved.*

Doc Sweaney Delivered Me.

— A Guest at a Party in D.C.

In the 1970's when I was living in Washington, D.C., one of my friends was dating a Georgetown graduate student. She told me that he was from Kansas City. Feeling nostalgic for a Missouri conversation, I introduced myself to the young man at my friend's next party. I told him that I was from Northwest Missouri, that I had been raised in a small town north of St. Joe. He said, although he grew up in Kansas City, he had spent summers at his grandparents who also lived in a small town north of the city, and that as a matter of fact he had been born there.

I asked him, "What town?" He answered, "Craig."

By then, I was curious and asked him, "What is your mother's family name?"

He said, "Haer."

I thought to myself, "Well, that makes sense if they were from Craig." I then said, "Do you know the name of the doctor who delivered you?"

He gave me a strange look, now really paying attention to me for the first time. This question was not your normal party chatter but he obliged by saying, "Doc Sweaney."

My friend started laughing, amazed. She said, "You know I have no idea of the name of the doctor who delivered me."

It seems if a couple went through pre-natal care and childbirth with my father at the helm, they never forgot him, and they told their children about the experience.

I've been told so many fun birthing stories:

A young expectant father nervous with the birth of his first born called Dad very excited. His wife's contractions had started.

Dad said, "Meet me at the office."

The soon-to-be father responded, "Should I bring my wife with me?"

Irene Derr, who had struggled with infertility for many years, came to see Dad for a routine office visit in 1953. Irene told me Dad called her the next day. She never forgot his words: "Irene, you need to call Iris. She has some maternity clothes to loan you."

Bill Richards, a month older than me, shared that he and his older siblings, David and Susan, were born in St. Joe. But, by the time his mother was pregnant with his younger brother Bob, her doctor told her that the Richards had a very good doctor in Oregon and that she should use him. As a result, Dad delivered the last of Ed and Fern's children at Fairfax Hospital—Bob was the 1000th baby to be born there.

Childbirth is a shared experience between the mother, father, baby and deliverer. Under Dad's care, this bonding experience began in his Oldsmobile with the trip to Fairfax. He would drive the expectant mothers to the hospital in his car, and the fathers would follow in their own car. This trip was never a calm, normal, experience.

Dad who travelled the road many times a day had it memorized; the farms along the way represented mileposts in his mind. He would time the soon-to-be mother's contractions as he drove the road by mentally calculating the distance between the farms. If the next contraction came too soon, before enough distance had been travelled, he sped up the car.

Pretty Yvonne—former Holt County Fair royalty—had married her high school sweetheart, Paul Markt, and she worked for Dad throughout her pregnancy with her daughter Karma. During her first trimester, she suffered from severe morning sickness and had doubts about whether she could continue working. Dad told her she just had to get through the next three months. He quipped, "Put on some lipstick, and you'll feel better." She responded, "I can't. The smell will make me throw-up." Sure enough though, like magic, she felt better after the first trimester was over.

When it came time to go to the hospital, her husband Paul called Dad at her very first contraction. Dad and Yvonne left for Fairfax in his car. From years of experience in delivering first babies, Dad knew that there would be time before the baby would arrive. Teasing Yvonne as he always did, he drove by way of Big Lake, a very scenic route but a very indirect one requiring the anxious new mother to be in the car for at least an extra thirty minutes.

Mrs. Jack Greene moved away from Oregon fifty years ago but recently wrote me:

Jack and I remember Doc Sweaney well. He delivered our second baby – Kelli. Yes, we made an early morning "wild" trip to Fairfax Hospital in ice and snow on Nov. 28, '57. I was in the back seat wondering if we would make it and thinking maybe I should have ridden with Jack. But all went well and she was born around noon...By the way, when he first examined me during my pregnancy, he stepped out of the room for a second and I fainted and fell off the table. What a shock! No harm done though. He got me back on the table and continued.

For Martha O'Connell making the trip in January of 1954 for the birth of her son Randy, the drive was even more eventful. They were just a few miles from Fairfax when dogs ran in front of the car. Dad swerved to miss them and lost control of the car. They landed in a ditch. Martha remembers the scene vividly: "The car and your dad's medical bag overturned. Pills were everywhere. Your dad climbed out of the car and waved down the next car telling them that 'There's a pregnant woman here that I need to get to the hospital.'" The passer-by picked them both up and took them to Fairfax Hospital. They arrived so that Randy could be born in the hospital delivery room.

But it is Bette Williams' story that I remember best. Dad smoked cigars while driving. He only enjoyed this habit in his car. Mom did not want him to smoke "those things" in the house, but he really enjoyed a good Cuban cigar. As Bette tells the story:

DR. SWEANEY AND PATIENT IN WRECK ON ICY PAVEMENT

From the Fairfax Forum:

Dr. I. F. Sweaney of Oregon, on the way to the Fairfax Community Hospital with a patient Tuesday morning, lost control of his car and it turned over, landing on its top. Neither the doctor nor his patient, Mrs. Arthur O'Connell of Oregon, was injured.

When near the Fred Smith place, about two miles south on Highway 275, Dr. Sweaney swerved his car a bit to avoid hitting some dogs on the pavement. The highway was slick because of the freezing mist. The car went to the shoulder, turned over on the top and slid down the shoulder a short distance before it stopped. It was damaged to the extent of about $400, but neither of the occupants was hurt.

Mrs. Joe Straub, employee of the hospital, came along on her way to work and brought Dr. Sweaney and Mrs. O'Connell to the hospital.

Holt County Sentinel, January 22, 1954

Kid, Doc and I were riding together with Russ following behind in our car. Of course, I am in labor not really paying attention to anything that is happening around me. Doc asked if I would care if he smoked a cigar. At that point, I was long past the point of caring about something so trivial. So, I said go ahead.

Doc said, "Can you get me one? I left them in the pocket of my coat. It's in the backseat."

So, Bette obligingly climbs over the seat to get the cigar. Russ, in the car behind, sees Bette, panics because he thinks she is getting in the back to have the baby. They made it to Fairfax and Bette gave birth to her third son, Bill. Bette did not mention if Dad smoked the cigar.

The women never forgot those rides.

Phyllis Narans, recounted another birthing story. Although she did not work in the office full time, Phyllis was there one day when she was needed. She was not an O.B. nurse. However, all her nursing skills were required when a young woman, not from Oregon, walked into the office seeking help – she was in labor, premature labor.

She was not a regular patient and no one on the staff knew her. Dad was on his way back from his routine of hospital visits and house calls in the northern part of the county. Phyllis had the telephone operator flag him as he drove through Mound City. He told the operator to tell Phyllis that he would be there as soon as he had a sandwich. Phyllis yelled, "Tell him to get here right now." Phyllis had to deliver the baby, a very difficult premature delivery because the baby was turned the wrong way.

When Dad walked in a bit later it was quite the scene. Phyllis, a little harried and overwhelmed, was wrapping the baby in a towel, and the unknown mother was resting on the delivery table. Doc immediately made plans to take the baby to Fairfax Hospital where there was an incubator. They were almost out the door with the baby before someone remembered the mother. After the day his staff had had, they just laughed and laughed.

No one remembers the name of the woman, or what happened to her or the baby, but they never forgot Phyllis yelling at the telephone operator and Dad's words.

Dad delivered only one set of twins. They just happened to be Mrs. Narans' grandchildren. When the first little girl was delivered, Dad checked the baby and then looked. He said to the tired mother, "I don't think you are through yet." There was a second little girl. He went to the waiting room and told Everet Narans, "I got it started and didn't' know how to stop it."

Dad with his twins.

He had always said that he would deliver his first set of twins at no cost. So, the twins' delivery did not cost the Narans' family. Dad told Mrs. Narans, "You might know we would keep it in the family."

All was not lightness and fun. Yvonne remembers the day that Dad lost both a mother and child. If she still remembers the woman's name, she did not share it with me. She said Doc came back to the office, did not say anything, just went into his room, closed the door, and sat by himself for hours.

Many of the pictures that I have of my father show him with one of the children that he delivered. Mom wrote behind one picture, "One of the many babies Frank delivered. Precious memories." No names, just the picture.

Left: Doc with baby on knee and stethoscope. An especially sweet photgraph of Dad holding a baby. The baby is clearly intrigued by the stethoscope!

Below: Lou Ann with stethoscope in her ears. Lou Ann mimics Dad by holding a stethoscope to Randy Gillenwater's chest. I guess the old adage that we learn from watching our parents held true for Lou Ann. She later became a nurse practitioner in Marin County, California.

Bottom: Mrs. Noland with Doc, clipping of birth notice, Doc in scrubs with newborn. Dad holding Kelton Noland minutes after his birth. Floris Noland in Dad's office before Kelton was born. (courtesy of Floris Noland) Kelton's birth announcement in the Holt County Sentinel on February 13, 1953.

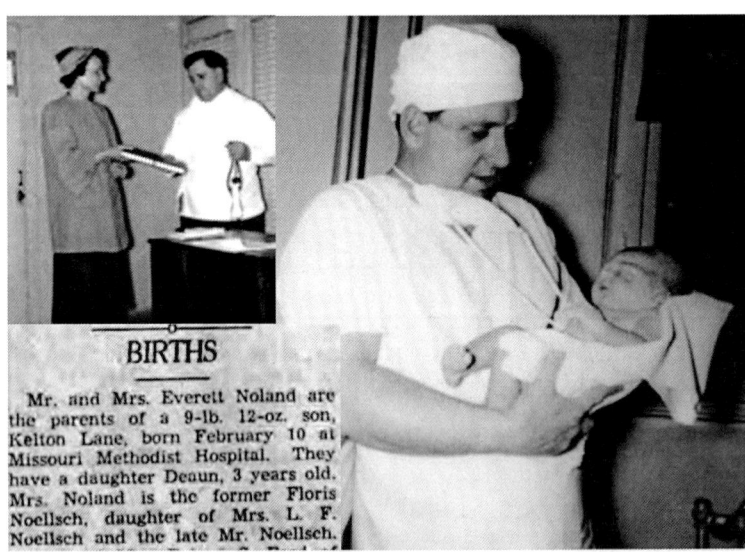

BIRTHS

Mr. and Mrs. Everett Noland are the parents of a 9-lb. 12-oz. son, Kelton Lane, born February 10 at Missouri Methodist Hospital. They have a daughter Deaun, 3 years old. Mrs. Noland is the former Floris Noellsch, daughter of Mrs. L. F. Noellsch and the late Mr. Noellsch.

OREGON'S MARCH OF DIMES

I remember walking from the old brick three-story grade school building downtown to Doc Sweaney's office for immunizations. We walked class by class, in order of higher to lower grades.

— Dorothy Richards Abbott, 2012

It has been more than a half a century since the word polio caused terror in the United States. Polio not only resulted in paralysis of the limbs but fear of the disease paralyzed the population. We look at posters featuring crippled children as artifacts from an earlier time. "Polio Summers" announcing closed swimming pools and warnings about too much exercise now seem quaint. It is difficult to imagine the fear that inspired these posters.

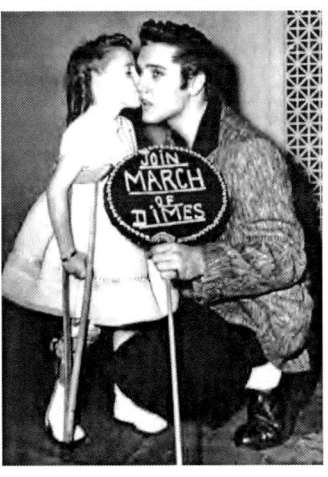

Elvis Presley kissed by March of Dimes Poster Child Joanne Kelly. (www.elvisinfonet.com/ interview_joannekelly.html)

It was this fear, however, that drove Americans to participate in the March of Dimes, the largest grass-roots volunteer effort of the post-World War II years. The March of Dimes was sponsored by the

POLIO

It was the robber of hope for a generation, several generations of children. There were diseases, and scientists will chart them, that were more devastating, affecting more children, more deadly than polio. But polio left kids crippled, and that was an image that this big strong postwar country simply couldn't abide. We had children lining up in wheelchairs, in iron lungs, whose very vitality and everyone's hope for their future was allayed right at the most critical time in their childhoods. And that's why polio seemed like such a horrible scourge, far more so than any number of other diseases or accidents that, any way you want to measure it, were more deadly and were fatal. And the image of a child in an iron lung is about as tearful and wrenching as we could imagine at that time, and any time certainly in this century. There were many other diseases that were bad for America, but polio broke its heart.

— Mark Sauer, polio survivor

from *A Paralyzing Fear*, an Emmy Award winning documentary

National Foundation for Infantile Paralysis. This foundation was the brainchild of polio victim President Franklin Roosevelt. It was a private, non-profit, organization. In an age before government-funded research grants, the National Foundation for Infantile Paralysis revolutionized medical research, fundraising, and the perception of disease in America. By adapting new methods first used by advertising agencies, the foundation mobilized communities to play a role in the crusade against polio. Celebrities and politicians lent their faces and names to the cause.

The campaign used striking images to open American's hearts and pocket books. Many patients with polio were unable to breathe because the virus paralyzed muscle groups in the chest. Patients with this condition were placed in a tank respirator known as an iron lung. Along with pictures of cute children walking with the aid of braces, pictures of patients in iron lungs became the symbol of the dreaded disease.

Holt County, like the rest of America, embraced this effort to raise money to find a cure. People in Northwest Missouri were well aware of the random nature of the disease. Polio struck the county in 1952 and 1953. The Missouri State Board of Health required physicians to report all cases of communicable diseases

Publicity photo showing the use of the iron lung. Looking remarkably happy under the circumstances, I might add.

in Missouri counties. They still have records from the fifties for Holt County which show that in that first important year of Dad's practice, 1953, there were 877 cases of polio in Missouri and four cases in Holt County. In 1952, a young Holt County native, John Herr, died after surviving for a time with the aid of an iron lung. The fear of the disease was based on reality.

Holt County Sentinel, 1954.

All Holt County organizations raised dollars earmarked for the March of Dimes. The cause cut across the county's social structure. The Holt County Sentinel carried articles every week about March of Dimes fundraising activities. The efforts were led by civic leaders who joined others in Northwest Missouri to discuss fund-raising strategies. Men went to meetings, and women organized events. Supporting the fund raising efforts to fight polio consumed much of the collective energy of the community in the early fifties.

The American Legion Post, the American Legion Auxiliary, the Adelpha Club, and other local civic organizations sponsored fund raisers. Card parties were held at the It L. Do

First Christian Church Announcement, 1953.

roadhouse outside of town. The conservative First Christian Church gave money from its collection plate to the cause. It was certainly not typical for the church and the roadhouse to work together, but fighting polio was more important than any differences.

Holt County Sentinal, January 1953.

In 1956, Dad launched a program to inoculate county children with the revolutionary breakthrough: the Salk vaccine. Many in

Holt County Sentinal, January 30, 1953.

Holt County of this generation remember their march from the Oregon school to Dad's office to receive their first polio inoculation.

The march of students started from the old brick Oregon school located five blocks from the town square. The students lined up by class, eighth graders to first graders. In each of the student's pocket was a dime. It was to be donated at Doc Sweaney's office and added to all the other dimes in America that had helped make this day possible.

The teachers had their hands full trying to organize the procession. The girls in their pretty dresses, their sashes tied in bows behind them, were much more manageable than the crew-cut boys. As the march proceeded down the first hill, a group of the boys were talking—none of them wanted to get a shot. Jim Kurtz

John Herr died December 29, 1952.

remembers that one of them got a bright idea: if they could not pay for it, they would not have to have a needle stuck in their arm. It is amazing how quickly dimes can be lost. By the time the group started up the next hill, not one of the boys could locate his dime.

They reached the top of the second hill, moved past the jail and the old courthouse, and marched across the west side of the town square into Dad's office. Mrs. Narans met them at the door and started collecting the dimes. I don't know how any of the boys had the courage to tell her that he had lost his dime. You just did not mess with Mrs. Narans. She would have none of that nonsense. She just went to her purse, got out a dollar, and paid their bill. That stopped the boys' rebellion. They lined up, very orderly, in the waiting room to enter Dad's inner office for their life-saving vaccination.

Left: *Holt County Sentinel, January 15, 1954.*

Above: *These students in their first grade float at the 1953 Fall Festival would have participated in "The March of Dimes" from the school to Dad's office.*
(courtesy of Gary Kurtz)

The vaccination was delivered by a non-disposable syringe—needles were removable and replaceable. In the haste to move the children through the process as quickly as possible, one needle was not secured tightly enough and broke off in a child's arm. His screams could be heard throughout the small office.

David Richards and his classmates were waiting to receive their immunizations when they heard those screams. David, now a professor of psychology at a college in New York, remembers:

I still talk about Doc Sweaney's immunization lineup in classes when the topic is conditioned anxiety. It was bad enough waiting in line and hearing the cries of other children as they received their shots, but the scream of the kid after the needle broke off was terrifying. For decades after this, I had such a fear of needles that I almost passed out once after one of those pinprick-in-the-finger blood tests. Only after I developed medical issues where I got shots and blood drawn on a regular basis did I get over my needle fears (not that I like it, though).

I Relied On Just Ten Drugs.
Two Of Them Were Cough
Syrup And Aspirin.

— *Dr. Harold Kretzing*

I have learned much about health care in the 1950's. I marvel at how primitive it now seems. People died, but of course people still die today. Practicing medicine during the fifties required a personal touch. There just weren't that many effective drugs or proven treatments. When Doc had no other treatment, he went to his safe to bring out the special medicine: sugar pills. He stored the placebos in his office safe along with controlled substances such as morphine.

Dr. Harold Kretzing, a retired family physician in Carlisle, Pennsylvania, told me that when he graduated from medical school in the early sixties, he relied on just ten drugs; two of them were cough syrup and aspirin. Dr. Kretzing may have been being a little facetious, but many pharmacology advances were still on the distant horizon. Among other issues, medical science had not yet established the relationship between high cholesterol, and other dietary factors, and the health of the heart and other vital organs.

Treatments that did exist were rather invasive. Medicine was administered by hypodermic needles. Basic surgery with anesthesia had been perfected, but recovery required a long period of convalescence; people stayed in the hospital for at least a week after even the most basic surgery. Women did not return home the next day after a baby was born, but were pampered for days by a hospital nurse.

I came to appreciate that in my father's world, the term health care was all about *care*. People could not always describe why, and medicine, clearly, was not always the reason, but "Doc Sweaney just made you feel better."

But my dad was not above tough love. On one occasion when he told a woman that she needed surgery to remove her gall bladder, she responded, "We just can't afford it." Doc looked at her, knowing full well that money was not an issue, he replied, "Can you afford a funeral?" She had the surgery.

When Dad wrote out a prescription, it was usually filled at Bill Rich's pharmacy. Rich's Pharmacy, like all businesses in town, was run on a charge and carry basis. Bill kept cards in a box by the cash register where he maintained a running tab for each family. When a person came into the store to fill his or her prescription, the family's card would be pulled out of the box. The new purchase with its cost would be hand-written on the card.

Each month, Dad stopped by Rich's. He checked to see if his prescriptions had caused any undue financial hardship for any of his patients and, if so, paid the drugstore bill.

Dad loved to tease and would not miss a chance to pull a joke on his fellow doctor. Remembering and laughing fifty-five years later Doctor Carpenter told me a story about him. Doc may not have really acted in the manner that he relayed to his friend—Sweaney men love to embellish a story—but it makes a good tale:

An old man down at Corning called me in for a house call. It was an old farm house with a pot belly stove. I gave him some pills. The next day the old man called your dad. Doc Sweaney had to make a second visit to our mutual patient. Your dad told me he did not even look at the pills. He just threw them in the pot belly stove and said, "Now let's make you well."

I would not be surprised though, if Dad prescribed the same pills to the patient before he left his house.

There were no medical specialists on the staff at the Community Hospital in Fairfax. All the doctors on staff were general practitioners, maybe with some surgical skills. Dad delivered babies, saw them through their childhood illness, and mended their broken bones when they fell from tree limbs. He removed appendices, gall bladders, and tonsils. He was at the bedside of seniors as they died. His shingle could have read: Gynecology, Obstetrics, Internist, General Surgery, Pediatrics, Psychiatry, and Geriatrics.

> In the opinion of the committee there is sufficient evidence to justify the conclusion that alcohol, tobacco, height, and weight are not concerned in the genesis of primary diastolic hypertension.
>
> — Position paper of several committees of the American Heart Association, 1957

On one level, it sounds good to have such personal care, but they just did not know that much. We now take so many of the advances in medical care of the last five decades for granted. We forget how recent they are. The medical profession's understanding of the complex system of the human body has grown exponentially. We now know that the food we eat, our weight, exercise, and our stress levels affect our health dramatically. I don't think the word lifestyle was even in the dictionary in 1960. In the fifties the only treatment they had for heart attacks was bed rest. The only determinate of survival was the severity of the attack.

Looking back at my childhood there seems to be an innocence to much of our lives. I want to hold onto that feeling, to romanticize it, but then I read the quote from the Heart Association in 1957. I am grateful for our increased understanding of medical issues and much of our technological advances. I carry the Sweaney genes in me and fight diabetes, high blood pressure, and obesity. I am glad that I live in today's world. However, I sometimes wonder if fifty years from now people will look back at our times and shake their head in amused amazement at our seemingly primitive care, clicking their tongues at our use of chemotherapy and radiation to treat cancer.

LIFE IN RURAL AMERICA

CHILD CHANGED HER NAME,
TOOK A LONG WALK IN C...

Lou Ann, three-year-old daugh...
of Dr. and Mrs. Frank Sweaney, w...
visiting in St. Joseph last week a...
she and a small cousin decided ...
go for a walk.

It was a long walk that covered...
three hours and a good many blocks,
but the two wanderers were located
by police after the alarmed relatives
sent out calls for assistance. Identity
of Lou Ann by the police was made
slightly more difficult because she
had decided to change her name th...
day for reason...

I Can't Imagine What Mom And Dad Went Through At That Time.

I often thought how awful for them to have to contend with a new baby after such a loss. He was their oldest of five children and I really believe that Dad and Mom never got over it but learned to live with it. But you know things do happen.

— Peggy LaHue Cox, 2012

We often picture family farms in a pretty, bucolic setting, but farms are places of business. Like factories they can sometimes be dangerous. Accidents required emergency medical treatment. Occasionally, these accidents are tragic.

James Carrol LaHue, only sixteen, was killed in June, 1952, driving a tractor onto a gravel road when it overturned in a drainage ditch. His father was following closely behind in a pickup but not close enough to prevent the accident. Peggy LaHue recently told me more about this sad story. Jimmy Carrol was her older brother although she never knew him. Peggy's mother was in the hospital recovering from her birth when her eldest son was killed. Leaving her new baby in the hospital to be cared for by nurses, Peggy's mom attended the funeral and buried her oldest son. Peggy remarks, "I can't imagine what Mom and Dad went through at that time."

Brad Bailey was in my first, second, and third grade class pictures. He was a bright, mischievous blonde boy. He was not in my fourth grade class picture. In the summer after third grade, Brad was killed in a grain silo accident playing on his family farm.

There were other dangers lurking as well. For those farming land in the Forbes and Forest City Missouri River bottoms, constant vigilance against rattlesnakes and copperheads was essential. Judy Ferguson Weiss remembers:

My aunt was bitten by a copperhead. They started to St. Joe to one of the hospitals, when they remembered that a new doctor had just recently moved to Oregon. Oregon being closer, they decided to try him. Doc sent them to the Fairfax hospital where they had one anti-venom kit.

It was a good thing that they contacted Dad, because the hospitals in St. Joe had no anti-venom kits in stock.

As Midwestern corn and soy bean production grew during the fifties and sixties, farms required laborers. In Holt County, this did not mean that migrant workers would be brought in for a harvest. Instead, farmers turned to local teenagers and young adults. In my youth, many kids in the county received their first paychecks by working on the farms.

When I was in junior high, I "walked beans," moving along the long row of beans on summer mornings, cutting down sunflowers and wild marijuana. Hemp had been used to make rope and was a cash crop in Holt County in the nineteenth century. It was now considered a weed. If not destroyed, it reduced the yield of a bean field. Farmers joked that it might have been more profitable to harvest the weed instead of the beans.

Our day would start right after sunup. We would begin work as soon as the morning dew on the beans evaporated, although the fields were often muddy from rain. As the morning progressed, it got hotter and our clothes stuck to our backs. Our day ended shortly after noon when the unrelenting sun made it impossible to continue.

In the 1960's, several farmers negotiated contracts with large seed companies such as Pioneer or Dekalb to grow seed corn. Crews of teenage girls pulled the tassels off corn—detasseling—which allowed the farmers to control pollination, and ensured that the seed corn was the exact hybrid the company wanted. We walked the long rows of the tall corn in bikini tops, our skin turned golden by the hot sun. These jobs were hard work, but they did not require the physical strength of being on a hay crew. That type of backbreaking work went to older teenage boys and young men.

Oregon was neither Mayberry nor Peyton Place, although it did have elements of both. There were premature deaths, unplanned pregnancies, school drop-outs and family scandals. But, we did have Sherriff Ramsey who watched over us, and there were several women who bordered on being "Aunt Bee."

Sexual activity was never openly acknowledged. It was only to be practiced in the bedrooms of married couples. However, people are people, and of course, pre-marital and extra marital sex occurred. In 1953, the State Health Statistics showed that there was one case of gonorrhea and four cases of syphilis in Holt County.

One night Dad was called to a home because a woman was having stomach pains. He went into the house leaving my mom in the car. It was one of her nights to accompany him. He came out a few minutes later and said, "That woman is in premature labor!" She never received any pre-natal care. The conservative couple had only been married a few short months and did not want to openly acknowledge their pre-marital activities; three very small triplets died that night. As far as I know, they would have been the only triplets in Holt County history.

There was a fair amount of drinking among the populace. Northwest Missourians had an unusual relationship with alcohol in the 1950s. "Sin" seemed to be determined by geography. Each state and municipality had laws that governed the sale of alcohol. Laws on the sale of beer changed as you left the Oregon city limits. If you wanted to purchase a beer on Sunday to enjoy with dinner, there was the It L. Do roadhouse right outside the city limits. I was never in the It L. Do, but I think people had a good time at this establishment. It was run by Ralph "Pood" Schaeffer. Everyone liked Pood. He was a funny guy. Mom told me about the night he needed medical attention. She remembered Pood saying, "You know that little house of 'ill repute' called the It L. Do? I own it." He arrived at the house with a severe burn, clearly in pain, but Mom said she never laughed so much in her life.

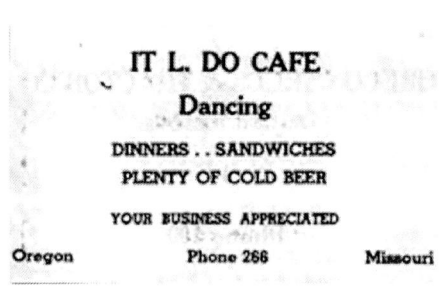

Advertisement from the 1954 Fall Festival Brochure.

Unfortunately, the drinking resulted in some closeted and not-so-closeted alcoholics. If the people who drank too much existed in the lower echelon of the defined society, then their drinking was openly acknowledged. For those of the upper echelons, talk about their use of alcohol was whispered. The liquor laws in Kansas and Nebraska made it easier to purchase beer, so teenagers growing up in Missouri would go across the river to drink. Driving back under the influence resulted in more than one serious car accident. Spousal and child abuse existed as well, often aggravated by too much alcohol. Behind the closed doors, corporal punishment of children sometimes went a little too far.

Mental illness was little understood by the medical profession. If a patient's depression was extreme enough to warrant treatment, he would be taken to the State Hospital in St. Joseph. The state hospital had originally opened its doors in 1874 as the Lunatic Asylum No. 2 but officially became the St. Joseph State Hospital in 1899. In the 1950s, it was still known as "No. 2" to citizens of Northwest Missouri. My schoolmates joked about sending someone to "No. 2."

The St. Joseph State Hospital (originally the State Lunatic Asylum No. 2) Historical psychiatric treatment devices from the St. Joseph State Hospital are housed at St. Joseph's Glore Psychiatric Museum. This museum chronicles the 130-year history of what was once known as the "State Lunatic Asylum No. 2." The Museum uses full-sized replicas, interactive displays, audio-visuals, and actual artifacts to illustrate the history of the treatment of mental illness. Recognized as "one of the 50 most unusual museums in the country," it is featured in Patricia Schultz's book 1,000 Places to See Before You Die in the USA and Canada (2007 Workman Publishing).

As a child, when we drove past the large fence-enclosed facility, I took deep breaths to ward off twinges of fear. I was reminded of those old movies, replayed on television in the fifties, in which women were wrongly hospitalized so that an in-law (usually an evil mother-in-law) could benefit financially. They always starred a beautiful woman such as Loretta Young.

I know another story, although I wish I did not. A woman arrived at Dad's office bleeding terribly after a botched self-induced abortion. We can only imagine what drove the conservative church-going woman to such lengths, but at that time her act was illegal. In denial, and almost bleeding to death, she just kept repeating "Doc, you know I would not do that." Dad patted her shoulder and said, "I know, I know." She lived. The change in abortion laws would not occur for several decades.

WE WERE GUIDED AND ENCOURAGED.

Our rewarding achievements are due to unselfish guidance, work, and encouragement of our parents, and community leaders; and we extend to them an appreciative "thank you."

— The 1961 Buccaneer, Oregon's Yearbook

The doctor's office was not the only place where Oregon children found support and care during the fifties. In my memory, the community was full of adults who nurtured their community's

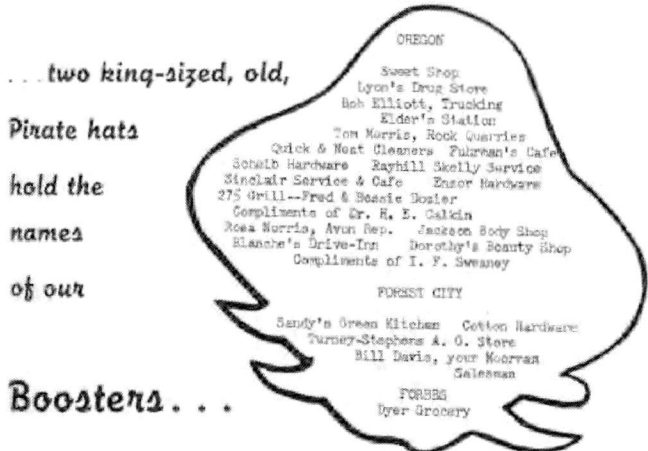

... two king-sized, old,

Pirate hats

hold the

names

of our

Boosters ...

OREGON
Sweet Shop
Lyon's Drug Store
Bob Elliott, Trucking
Elder's Station
Tom Morris, Rock Quarries
Quick & Neat Cleaners   Fuhrman's Cafe
Schalb Hardware   Rayhill Skelly Service
Sinclair Service & Cafe   Ensor Hardware
275 Grill--Fred & Bessie Dozier
Compliments of Dr. R. E. Calkin
Rosa Norris, Avon Rep.   Jackson Body Shop
Blanche's Drive-Inn   Dorothy's Beauty Shop
Compliments of I. F. Sweaney

FOREST CITY

Sandy's Green Kitchen   Cotton Hardware
Turney-Stephens A. G. Store
Bill Davis, your Koorran
Salesman

FORBES
Dyer Grocery

Community Boosters, Oregon Yearbook,
The 1952 Buccaneer.

children, and the business community openly supported school and community events boosting activities with financial support.

In particular, my classmates' mothers were part of my life, and I called them by their first names. It did not matter if the name was Fern, Mary, Dema Jo, Darlyne, or Millie, instead of Iris; I paid attention to their instructions and never sassed them.

When people think of 4-H, the images that often comes to mind are farm children raising animals for show. 4-H was not just for kids on farms, however, town children also learned from this program. Adults volunteered to teach children skills. I learned to boil an egg in a cooking class taught by Mary Ann Payne and to knit from Jane Ann Milne. I can still recite the pledge, "My Head to clearer thinking, My Heart to greater loyalty, My Hands to larger service, and My Health to better living for my Club, my Community, and my Country."

Each year, the 4-H kids were divided into teams to perform skits for "Share-the-Fun." These skits were incredibly competitive with winning skits advancing to regional and state competitions. They brought out the "stage-mother" in many women who spent a considerable amount time organizing teams, writing scripts, and directing children in these performances.

1953 Fall Festival Float (courtesy of Gary Kurtz).

Oregon's 4-H parents felt their rural charges needed some limited exposure to urban America and arranged a trip for the town's children to Chicago. Our group was heavily chaperoned by many mothers who counted our heads as more than fifty children boarded the train in St. Joe. In spite of all the chaperones, two boys free from the confines of their home tried to smoke cigarettes in the train's lavatory. They were caught by vigilant mothers watching out for just such an incident.

We saw the Windy City from a tour bus, viewing Chinatown and the tall buildings from its windows. It all looked a little intimidating to me. We left the bus briefly to tour a few landmarks such as McCormick Place and the Museum of Science and Industry. At the museum we lined up to enter the museum's featured exhibit: a captured World War II German submarine. Two Catholic sisters were in the line ahead of our small town group. I had never before seen a nun and found their habits much more interesting than the captured war artifact.

Nonie McGuire volunteered to lead the Girl Scouts. Lou Ann and I were in her brownie troop. We met in the basement of the building that housed the variety store.

Brownie Scout Troop — 1957-1958

Oregon Brownie Troop. Lou Ann is on the end of the first row in saddle shoes. (Carried in the Times Observer, Oct. 20, 2005)

AMERICAN LEGION
POPPY

The American Legion Auxiliary worked to educate children in the American political system and patriotic causes. Mom was very active in this group. Each spring the Auxiliary sponsored activities around a "poppy" theme. There was a state-wide poppy poster contest actively endorsed and encouraged by the school system. I can remember walking around the town square asking people to support veterans at VA hospitals. I gave them a poppy in exchange for their contributions. You were instructed to never ask someone to "buy" a poppy. It was always to be a donation. These, of course, were American Legion crepe-paper poppies, not the stiff, plastic, poppies of the rival V.F.W.

Later, when I was a teenager, the Legion Auxiliary sponsored "County Government Day" to teach youth about the local political structure and sent representatives to Girl's State, a state-wide honors program where girls learned to conduct mock elections for state officials. I won third place in the annual county-wide essay contest with my essay, "What I learned at County Government Day." When I was in high school I was a representative from Oregon to Girl's State. I realize now what an influence these programs had on my career choice to move to Washington, D.C. and work as a staff member and consultant for our country's legislative and executive branches of government.

In junior high, nice girls joined Rainbow Girls, the girl's service organization of the Masons and the Order of the Eastern Star. We wore formal gowns, performing a ritual that required us to kneel in the shape of a cross with our right hand on the left shoulder of the girl in front of us, singing the "Old Rugged Cross." I can still remember Pauline Kee, our adult chaperon, telling us, "If we walked our prettiest, sat our prettiest, and stood our prettiest, we would be the prettiest girls in the whole State of Missouri."

1953 Fall Festival Float. (courtesy of Gary Kurtz)

The men in our community volunteered their time to lead a very active Boy Scouts program and several boys in the community earned Eagle Scout recognition. Men such as Mickey McComb, who guided the local scouts for over fifty years, gave of their time to nurture boys. Boy Scouts attended Camp Geiger located on the bluffs above the Missouri River, two miles northwest of St. Joseph.

Adults: Glenn Waller, Mickey McComb, and Ben Kneale led a group to Philmont Scott Ranch. The Scouts are my contemporaries. (courtesy of Betty Waller)

As an honor, scouts were inducted into the tribe of Mic-o-Say where both men and boys studied American Indian lore. They created Indian costumes and re-enacted Indian dances. I remember helping my brother create his costume from a kit. We affixed the feathers to the head piece with glue, probably not the technique used by the original Indians in Northwest Missouri, the Sac tribe. The Mic-o-Say traditions may not have been authentic but generations of Northwest Missouri men and boys bonded through the experience.

Arnie Kreek remembers his Mic-o-Say costume constructed out of blue and white feathers:

One day Mom put on the feather bustle from my costume to entertain my little brother. When she danced around the house it scared the cat so much that it ran through the kitchen and jumped right through the screen on the screen door.

Boy Scouts in Mic-o-Say costumes at the Forest City Centennial Parade, 1957. (150 Years of Forest City, Missouri History)

There were several women's organizations devoted to creating opportunities for the town's children and improving the community. However, these clubs also enriched the lives of their members – mothers and wives whose focus otherwise, pretty much revolved around their children and husbands. The Adelpha Club, was affiliated with the General Federation of Women's Clubs (GFWC), while others, like Happy Homemakers may have been Oregon creations. Each club had a focus and a group of women who were brought together by friendship, neighborhood proximity, or shared values. There was a bit of social standing regarding club membership similar to the Junior League in some towns, although I do not think that there was ever a formal black-ball voting process to membership selection. Women gathered, usually once a month, in a member's home, the hostess serving lunch or dessert on her best china. In the business meeting, after a short devotional, they planned civic projects, but they also shared stories and advice. When we were packing up memories, we found the quilt blocks for a "Friendship" quilt in mom's closet. The blocks had been made during one of these club meetings. Each woman embroidered her signature on multiple quilt blocks, and then took a complete set home to be patch-worked into a quilt. Mom never had the time to complete this final stage.

The names on the blocks brought back memories—several of the women had died of cancer or other illnesses. I thought of women who through the years have united in church or civic organizations, nurturing each other, talking of their children, sharing life's joys and sorrows, and contributing at the same time to the social warfare of their community.

Everyone Could Tell You Where The Sweaneys Lived.

Go about three blocks down from Doc's office and turn left. You will see the big house on the corner lot at the end of the street.

— Just ask anyone

I lived in a neighborhood on the western edge of Oregon. Officially, Pine Street bordered it, but no one in Oregon could tell you where Pine Street was. Everyone in town, however, could tell you where the Sweaneys lived—even if they had to direct you by landmarks.

The neighborhood children climbed trees, got into scrapes, skinned knees, and played dress-up. We entertained ourselves by creating games and fantasies, our adventures limited only by the power of our imagination. In our world, older children got to lord over younger children. They decided which games we played and assigned roles. With her longer legs, Lou Ann ran faster, and I struggled to catch her. She frightened me with tales of haunted houses and bogey men. We emulated the town's teenagers and older children. Lou Ann pretended to be Jo Ann Kunkle adopting the older girl's name in her games or when she was afraid that she would be reprimanded. My sister's first mention in the press came when she gave Jo Ann's name in place of her own to the St. Joe police after getting lost in the city.

Our house and yard were the center of this neighborhood, so on warm summer nights all the neighbor kids gathered in the front yard. We played "Pig in my pen." I don't remember the rules of this game. It must have been a variation on hide-and-go-seek. I do know that the front porch was the pen and the "it" person would shout "Pig in my pen on Debby (or another name)" when someone was caught. Oregon people of my generation remember playing Pig in my pen and repeat the comment, "I loved that game."

CHILD CHANGED HER NAME, TOOK A LONG WALK IN CITY

Lou Ann, three-year-old daughter of Dr. and Mrs. Frank Sweaney, was visiting in St. Joseph last week and she and a small cousin decided to go for a walk.

It was a long walk that covered three hours and a good many blocks, but the two wanderers were located by police after the alarmed relatives sent out calls for assistance. Identity of Lou Ann by the police was made slightly more difficult because she had decided to change her name that day for reasons understood best by herself. When officers found the children, happily throwing rocks in a street, Lou Ann insisted she was Jo Ann Kunkel.

Holt County Sentinel,
Nov. 20, 1953.

When the weather turned colder, neighborhood games moved inside our house. We played "Murder in the Dark." I remember well the intricate rules we developed. We played it in the old living room. The game always started by the players drawing lots to determine who would be the murderer and who would be the detective. The detective left the old living room for the new living room behind the sliding doors. The lights were turned off and the murderer would attack and "kill" one of the other players. The victim would scream loudly and fall dead on the floor.

When we turned the lights back on, everyone would engage in setting the crime scene and planting clues for the detective. These clues would be based on props found in the room. We often used one of the many books from the book cases that lined the room as part of the staging. *The World Book Encyclopedias* were very useful in this regard. If my brother Jim was the murderer, the "J" book might be placed near the body—but we also planted false clues to lead the detective astray. Then, the detective was invited back into the room to solve the crime. We played multiple games in an evening with new detectives and victims.

Once, years later when we were adults and sitting around with our spouses, one of us suggested playing "Murder in the Dark." I don't think our spouses ever caught on to the rules of the game and only grudgingly participated.

Occasionally we left the protective cocoon of our neighborhood to play at another house in Oregon. Bill Rich, the pharmacist, had built a new house on the edge of town. Lou Ann and I were invited to play with his children Sue and David. We built bugs from pieces of the "Cootie Game." I shudder when I realize that we played a game where we essentially built "head lice."

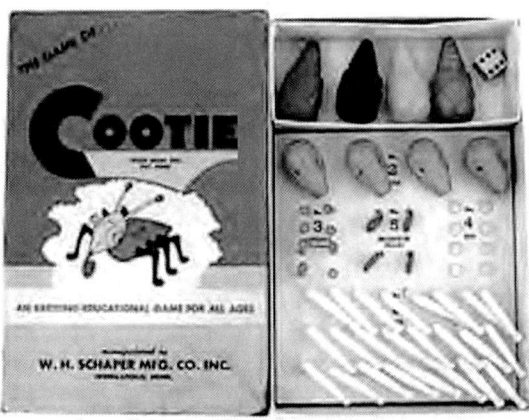

The Game of Cootie is a children's roll-and move tabletop game for two to four players. The object is to be the first to build a three dimensional bug-like object called a "cootie" from a variety of plastic body parts. Created by William Schaper in 1948, the game was launched in 1949 and sold millions in its first years. In 2003, Cootie was named the Toy Industry Association's "Century of Toys List."

http://en.wikipedia.org/wiki/CootieGame

Our house faced north. The street turned the corner on the west side. On that street were the Atkins, Jackson, and Planalp houses. Each house had kids of various ages that were part of our neighborhood.

The pavement ended after the Planalps and turned into an old dirt road. This road had once been the route from Oregon to Forest City but had long since been abandoned as the primary road. The old dirt road was used only to reach the farms out in that direction. For the kids in the neighborhood, this road was a source of numerous adventures.

Neighbors: Eric Planalp, Jim Jackson, Kevin Atkins, Don Planalp, Jim Sweaney. (photo courtesy of Don Planalp)

There was an old abandoned house on it. We were sure that it was haunted. I always walked quickly past it, but Lou Ann, more adventuresome, walked closer. I don't believe for an instant, however, that she would ever have thought of going inside.

I was Jim and Carry's older sister and felt responsible for them when Mom was gone. One day, Jim balked at my authority. It had been rainy the previous few days, but he wanted to go play on the Old Road. I told him he would get muddy and that rain water could be dangerous. His snappy response was, "I don't have to obey you."

But I got even. When Jim came home all covered with mud, I told him. "We have to talk." I opened one of Dad's medical books and said, "I just looked up typhoid. Everyone knows typhoid is carried by dirty water. We need to check your tongue." Jim stuck out his tongue.

I read out loud to him, "In typhoid fever the tongue becomes white coated like a fur." I looked at his tongue and said, "I don't know. I may see some white coating. We better keep an eye on it." At this point, Jim's tongue may not have been white but his face was pale. I caught him looking at his tongue several times over the next days.

In the *Box Car Children*, Gertrude Chandler Warner writes stories of four kids who run away after their mother dies because they are afraid of their grandfather. The kids set up home in an abandoned box car and have all sorts of independence and adventures. In the end, the children and grandfather are reunited and they realized how much he loves them. We reenacted these stories and variations on them next to a little stream off the Old Road. In our games, we could change our family pecking order. Carry, always a younger sister when she played with me, got to be "Jessie", the oldest girl in the story, when she played with our younger neighbors, Kevin, Kelly, and Kerry Beth Atkins.

On my last day in Missouri after my siblings and I had cleaned out Mom's house, and Grandma McCluey's suitcase sat on top of what I was shipping back east, I took a walk down the Old Road. It seemed much shorter now, perhaps because my legs were longer or maybe as a child I had been distracted by my fantasies. It did not take me long to reach its intersection with the paved road that now leads to Forest City. I think I picked out the plot of land where the haunted house once stood, and I moved quickly past. Twenty-five years had not completely erased my fear.

DICK SAID, "HERE, SPOT! COME AND GET THIS. THIS IS FOR YOU. RUN, SPOT, RUN."

— Life with Dick and Jane and Friends

Many of our adventures involved books. I saw Dick, Jane and Spot run in Mrs. Lark's first grade class, and from that moment I have enjoyed forming pictures in my mind from written words. There was a world beyond my somewhat confined borders, a world of intrigue, romance and knowledge. Through books, I developed a love for history and learned life lessons.

The old living room in our family home was lined with book cases. On one of the shelves, we had a set of *World Book Encyclopedias* covered in red and blue, with gold lettering. I learned the alphabet by arranging *World Books* by the letters printed on each book's spine.

All homes of the fifties in America seemed to have these books. World Book, Inc. had a smart marketing strategy: they hired teachers to sell their books during summer vacations. Parents wanted their children to do well in school so *World Book* capitalized on these dreams. Whenever a topic came up in our house, we pulled out a World Book to read about it. Mom cut out newspaper articles to add to the encyclopedias, tucking the articles into the appropriate book to keep the printed information current.

Later, books opened up an even larger world. Mom bought a Best Loved Girls' Books series subscription and I spent afternoons reading novels by Betty Cavanna. When I was in junior high, her books about teenage life such as *Angels on Skis* and *6 On Easy Street* told me about the exciting life that could be mine in a few years. Although, the career choices portrayed for girls seemed to be limited to the serving professions, the "Sue Barton" stories about young nursing students told me that girls could have careers. And of course there was Nancy Drew. I tested my analytical abilities against hers, but I could never equal her range of skills. She sent Morse code with tap shoes, picked locks with a bobby pin, and drove a roadster with her chums, Bess and George.

I spent many hours in the town library. In grade school, my favorite books were from the *Childhood of Famous Americans* series of highly fictionalized biographies of famous people—I remember the blue and orange covers. They started with stories about prominent figures as children, and their accomplishments as adults were presented in the last two chapters. Each had a caption under the title identifying the famous person such as, *Dan Webster: Union Boy* or *Thomas A. Edison: Young Inventor*. In the 1800s, Parson Weems helped form America's national identity with stories about George Washington cutting down the cherry tree. My orange and blue books were in this tradition.

I checked out Laura Ingalls Wilder's books. Fifty years later, I still pick up one of the *Little House* books to read when I need to escape from a dreary, rainy Sunday. I know the order of the Ingalls' family migration through the Midwest, still hate Nellie Olson, and secretly wish for a romance with Cap Garland or Almanzo Wilder. I bought business cards recently and Laura's pretty card that she presented to Almanzo in the *Little Town on the Prairie* came to my mind.

The town librarian reinforced standards by charging two cents a day for an overdue book. Mom was very upset if we carelessly let a book become overdue. We could always renew it for another two weeks so there was absolutely no excuse to ever have to pay a library fine. The librarian also felt a responsibility for the moral upbringing of the town's children. Lou Ann ran afoul of her once when she tried to check out *Of Mice and Men*. The librarian was concerned about its adult content, but Mom sent a note back giving Lou Ann permission to read any book.

At one point when I was in junior high I forgot Mom's position on censorship. Lou Ann, in high school, brought home a bestselling, somewhat scandalous, novel of the fifties, *Harrison High*. One night, as she was reading in place of helping me wash the evening dishes, she dramatically exclaimed "I just can't put it down." When I asked her what the book was about, she just said "high school students" with that oldest-child-superior-attitude implying I was just too young to understand...Of course, the minute she put it down and was not around, I found the book and started reading it. It contained passionate but not very graphic sex between football players and cheerleaders.

Lou Ann found me reading it and made me feel as if I was committing a cardinal sin. She said that she would not tell Mom if I cleaned up her room. Taking a break from my busy effort to sweep Lou Ann's floor, I went to the stairs and heard Lou Ann and Mom talking. She was laughing and telling Mom how she had tricked me. I was mad at my older sister for years over that joke—but I also have a profound respect for my mother's open-mindedness. I found *Harrison High* at a used book store in Pennsylvania recently and bought it. In the forty-seven years since I first read it, it had become so tame.

Ann Noellsch and I read *Gone with the Wind* in eighth grade. Nothing can rival the obsession of two thirteen- year-old girls. I read the book so many times that I can still say passages by heart. We talked about the book for hours. It had everything—history and sex. I didn't know details about what happened after Rhett carried Scarlett up the red-carpeted stairs, but I knew it was exciting, wonderful, and forbidden.

Lou Ann, attending William Jewell College in suburban Kansas City, invited us both to stay for a week-end in her college dorm and most importantly to go into the city to see a revival of the Academy Award-winning movie. After the movie, Ann and I spent weeks discussing which of Scarlett's dresses were the prettiest. Ann liked the green dress (made in desperation from curtains) that was designed to seduce Rhett. But I thought that she looked really beautiful in black—which she wore a lot because so many people in the movie died. One day, feeling cranky, and tired of the endless discussions I said, "*Gone with the Wind* is not the Bible."

She looked at me aghast and said, "You cannot possibly feel about the book the way I do!"

Look! Up In The Sky!

— Preamble to Superman

Lou Ann, Jim, Carry, and I were born in the years following World War II, clearly making us part of the large generation of baby boomers that still dominate so much of American culture.

Television tied us to baby boomers across our nation. We were among the first in Oregon to get a large black-and-white TV set. Judy Ferguson Weis recalls that it was only the second television that she had ever seen. Mom was always concerned that we would watch too much TV. On Saturday mornings, we had to turn off the set immediately after *Fury* ended at 10:30 a.m. Then, we were expected to help with chores around the house. She would write jobs on pieces of paper, put the papers in the sugar bowl, and we had to select a chore from the bowl.

Since the day Fess Parker put on Davy Crockett's coonskin cap, merchandisers have tapped into the large consumer pool of boomers. Advertisers used television to create a national culture. American children all demanded Kool Aid, Wonder bread, and Ovaltine. I begged for candy cigarettes packaged to mimic the brand names advertised in cigarette commercials. Across America, parents bought their kids hula hoops.

Watching pioneer television was an experience that American children of my generation shared. We all knew that the world pictured on the television set did not match the reality of our lives. Fathers, unlike Jim Anderson in the popular television show, did not always know best. Up in the sky, there really were only birds and airplanes, not Superman. And, our country still is trying to make the "American Way" include more truth and justice.

My husband Jim grew up in New York City. His childhood environment could not have been more different from mine. A couple of years ago we bought the complete set of the original *Adventures of Superman* episodes starring George Reeves, on DVD. Although, we had first watched them more than a thousand miles apart, he in his home in Brooklyn and I in rural Missouri, we both remembered that coal under the pressure of Superman's strength could become a diamond. It was fun, in the words of the Lone Ranger, to return to those "days of yesteryear." We laughed together, marveling at the fact that adults could be so clueless. Every child in America could figure out that Clark Kent looked exactly like Superman, but Perry White, Lois Lane, and Jimmy Olson never caught onto his secret identity.

It Was "I Before E Except After C."

— Educational rhyme

I started grade school in 1958. In the fall, Lou Ann and I walked the seven blocks to the school, scattering piles of leaves and enjoying the noise they made beneath our feet. I wore pretty dresses with a sash tied in a big bow in the back. Mom tied the bow for me each morning. She knew how to do it so that it stood up, almost as if it had been starched into place. If I came home with a lopsided bow, she knew that the sash had come untied during the day and another person without her expertise had tied it.

In the winter, our neighbor Lowell Planalp would drive us to school with his daughters Susan and Sally. I envied the farm kids who came to school in big yellow buses. At lunch time, Lowell picked us up to take us home for a hot lunch. I have a clear memory of one lunch at home in January of 1961. We watched the television newscast from Washington, D.C. as John F. Kennedy was sworn in as President. I do not recall hearing, "Ask not what your country can do for you....," but I remember the nation's capital looked very cold and wintry.

The farm kids got to stay at school, eating their sack lunches in a large group and playing games conducted by Mrs. Lark or Miss Markt.

Ann Noellsch, one of the 'lucky' farm kids, told me that on special occasions her mother packed fried chicken in her brown paper sack.

In 1958, small communities still existed in the rural areas around Oregon. Some of them still had one-room school houses where neighboring families sent their children to be educated through the eighth grade. These kids were then scheduled to join the Oregon school system in high school. When we were in the sixth grade, the State of Missouri closed Highland, Monarch, and Richville schoolhouses, and our class grew with students from these schools.

Peggy LaHue remembers spending her first five school years at the one-room Highland School. Her memories are of playing Handy Over, Red Rover, and dodge ball during recess. Families maintained a close-knit community spirit and met for cookouts and cake walks. Children entertained with Christmas and Thanksgiving plays. Peggy remembers her mother bringing hamburgers with lots of onions on them to her and her brother for lunch and then from time to time, she brought a big bowl of bread pudding for all the students. In the bigger Oregon school, these traditions fostered by one-room schools had already been abandoned.

Larger communities such as New Point and Forbes built large school buildings in the style of the Oregon school. Each of these buildings had a gym in the basement with basketball hoops. Some of Holt County's best basketball players got their start shooting hoops in these basements. An old brick school building, doors closed long ago to students, still stands in the middle of a field near New Point. When I drove past it, I thought of the old school buildings in Washington, D.C. that had been renovated into very expensive condominiums. The high ceilings and interesting angles of the New Point school building would also make great apartments but there would certainly be no demand for such homes in Holt County.

A little over fifty children were born in Oregon and its immediate vicinity in 1952. Most of us started first grade together and stayed in the same classes until we graduated from high school. Our class never exceeded the fifty-seven students in our freshman high school class. For Oregon, this was a large class.

Oregon Grade School 1958

In Oregon, you are remembered forever by who was in your class. We played a key role in each other's lives until we graduated from high school. We attended the same classes, had the same teachers, and knew each other's families.

I recently came across our third grade class picture. I knew instantly that we were in the third grade because Miss Mary Markt was the teacher. She taught Oregon third graders for decades. Long before physical fitness became the norm, Miss Markt made us go outside for recess in all temperatures. We played Work-up, a variation on baseball where players moved to new positions on the diamond when a person struck out.

Miss Markt's 1960-1961 third grade class. The author is the third person in the second row.

Miss Markt's teaching style, like many of our grade school teachers, reflected the traditions of the one room school house. She required all her students to bring a three-ring binder to school and we added papers to it throughout the school year. On the first page in all our binders we wrote a poem that she had recited, "The Goldenrod." I decorated the margins of my page with yellow flowers.

My father's handwriting could have been the basis for the many jokes about a doctor's handwriting. When Lou Ann was in the second grade, Dad wrote a permission slip for her to attend a field trip. Miss Sommer, the second grade teacher for all Oregon students during the fifties, studied it for a while and said, "I guess you can go." This was from a person who was comfortable discerning childish scrawls.

Miss Markt taught us cursive writing. Her letters written with chalk on the black board almost reached the level of calligraphy. We modeled our letters after hers and were strictly graded on our penmanship. When I take my time, I still write my capital "S" in that graceful style.

We diagramed sentences. First, we drew a line on the paper. In the center of the line, we drew a mark. We wrote the noun on one side of the mark and the verb on the other side. Qualifying adjectives and adverbs were indicated by connecting slanted lines to the noun or the verb. We learned the idiosyncrasies of the English language by rhymes: "Good, Better, Best, Never let it rest, until your good is better and your better is your best." And most importantly, "I before E except after C, or when it spells A as in neighbor and weigh."

Many of the teachers like Miss Markt started teaching in the Oregon school system when they were in their twenties and stayed through several generations of children. My siblings and I all had Miss Sommer for second grade and Miss Markt for third. Mrs. Shaeffer taught Lou Ann in first grade, but she retired before I and my younger brother and sister started school, so we were ushered into school days by Mrs. Lark.

Miss Markt listens as her third graders read their weekly readers. (Oregon Yearbook, The Buccaneer, 1966).

The bond created by this continuity is amazingly strong. At my mother's funeral, several of these women made a special effort to visit us after the family luncheon—they wanted to see the Sweaney kids that they had taught.

Before she married, my mother had been a one-room school teacher at the Stone School close to her home in the Ozark foothills. Like Miss Markt, she learned to write when penmanship was valued. Mom's handwriting was so beautiful her letters were a pleasure to read not only for their content but their style. Now I treasure them for both reasons—but her artistry is worthy of framing.

Iris when she was teaching in a one-room school house before her marriage.

She also had a collection of sayings that she used as educational tools, but now they were for her children not her students. The sayings always spoke to me of an earlier time and brought to mind images of blackboards, barefoot students, and boys in overalls. I pictured Mom as Laura Ingalls Wilder teaching at the Brewster School in the *Little House* books.

I remember her sayings so clearly. On windy March days, I'll recite,

The March wind blows the washing
And twists it on the line.
It pushes me along the street,
And steals Jane's hat and mine.
But, I don't mind the weather,
It makes me want to sing,

For I know it's pushing winter out
And making room for spring.

There was also a poem that started,

I meant to do my work today,
But a brown bird sang in the apple tree,
And a butterfly flitted across the field,
And all the leaves were calling me...

Or, my personal favorite:

This old world we live in
Is mighty hard to beat,
You get a thorn with every rose
But aren't the roses sweet.

Whenever, I see graffiti, I think, "Foolish names like foolish faces are always seen in public places." I have absolutely no idea what this means, but it is on the tip of my tongue when I see the results of spray paint on an embankment.

After Mom died, when we were emptying Dad's safe, we found a poem that she had copied for my brother. Jim like many McCluey's before him was losing his hair.

God is great
God is fair
He gave some men brains,
the others hair.

King James And Uncle Sam Lived Side By Side.

The settlement of the county and the organization of the first churches were almost contemporaneous.

— The History of Holt and Atchison Counties, 1882

Families went to church on Sundays. It was part of the culture. There was nothing else to do during this time since stores were closed. Many families attended a specific church because their ancestors had helped build it. In Oregon, the churches were all Protestant. In neighboring Forest City, there was a Catholic church. One Catholic family had children in the Oregon School system. When the Great Society brought school lunches into the public school system, the school board honored "the meatless Friday" religious tradition by ensuring that macaroni and cheese was served on Fridays.

Mom's Scottish Presbyterian heritage had been modified by exposure to Southern Baptists. The First Christian Church followed its teachings of baptism by immersion and a God who was present in everyday life. It was the best fit for my mom's faith. Earl Wilson invited our family to the First Christian Church very soon after Mom and Dad moved to Oregon. Earl was an Elder. He was a local farmer and also known for his inventions and problem solving skills.

144 | UNPACKING MEMORIES

One year the church had a revival planned. During the week of the revival, however, new power lines were being laid between Oregon and Forest City and electricity was cut off. Earl got a tractor and rigged it up to a generator with pulleys and belts. Church leaders said "The lights never flickered once" during the whole week long revival.

Judy Ferguson Weis remembers that the first time Mom came to church she entered on the north side. Years later, people still remember that she always sat in the second row on this side of the church. That first Sunday she carried me in her arms—I was only about three weeks old—and Lou Ann ran ahead into the adjoining kitchen. When she saw that the room was empty, she came back to Mom and announced loudly to the entire congregation, "No one at home!"

Mom became a member of the BBC Class (Build Better Christians), and for the better part of the following forty years she was its teacher. Dad was made a church officer although he seldom attended church on Sunday mornings since he was almost always at the Fairfax Hospital visiting his patients at the time the old church bell rang.

Merrill Ferguson, Judy's father, was the minister. He became a close supportive friend of our family. Merrill's name was mentioned in many of the obituaries printed in the *Holt County Sentinel* during the time period. He conducted many of the funeral services in town even for those who did not attend church. He had strong pastoral gifts and used them for the good of the community. I remember his love and concern.

Steve Burrier was one of the popular athletes in my class, a future "Big Man on Campus." I, of course, was a serious student. Our paths in school did not often cross. However, our families went to the same church. He recently wrote me of his recollections, so similar to mine, of being supported by adults at the church:

Remember the Wednesday afternoon youth groups at our church? And of course my dad was an Elder in the church and Mom taught high school Sunday school when we were very young.... Then a few years later Mom and Dad taught our youth groups on Sunday evenings. They were held at our house on the farm. Those times sure don't seem all that long ago to me.

No one worried about the concept of "separation of Church and State." King James and Uncle Sam somehow seemed to be related. On February 19, 1960, the Oregon High School burned. Since high school students moved from room to room, their classes needed to be held in one building, so their classes were moved into the grade school. I was in second grade at the time.

Since churches were the only other large buildings in town, they opened their doors and housed the grade school classes. First and second grades met in the basement of the Christian Church. Other grades were held in the Methodist and the Presbyterian Churches. In the fall, our second grade moved upstairs and met on the first floor of the Christian Church. School officials acknowledged in a *Holt County Sentinel* article that the arrangements were "far from satisfactory, but under the circumstances are the most logical."

At the Fall Festival in 1953, the BBC class participated by building a float.

1953 Fall Festival Float. (courtesy of Gary Kurtz)

Members of the class dressed in period costumes from the late nineteenth century. Mom is in a black dress at the end of the second to the last row in the picture. Merrill is delivering the message. I remember many people who would have been on this float. They were supportive players in my youth. The float, based on an old hymn, won the grand prize that year:

Church in the Wildwood

There's a church in the valley by the wildwood
No lovelier place in the dale.
No spot is so dear to my childhood
As the little brown church in the vale.

Chorus:
Oh, come to the church by the wildwood.
Come to the church in the dale.
No place is so dear to my childhood
As the little brown church in the vale.

The Month Of May, 1960.

O, the month of May, the merry month of May,
So frolic, so gay, and so green, so green, so green!

— Thomas Dekker, The Merry Month
of May, 1599

In Grandma's suitcase, there was a small yellow Kodak envelope containing photographic negatives. I held them to the light. I could see the outline of people on them but I was not able to make out the ghost-like images. I took them to a professional photography store and had them digitized. There, before me were images taken in May 1960 that I had never seen.

My family is in our yard playing. Dad is obviously taking the pictures. He liked cameras. Several old ones could be found in one of our closets. He must have been home for a short break between seeing patients. The Olds is in the driveway.

Mom must have been working in the yard. She is in jeans. This fact alone amazed me. I never remember Mom wearing pants when I was young. It would be many years later, when it became acceptable for women of her generation to wear pantsuits, before she would go out in public in anything but a dress. Lou Ann, a little independent from family life by this time, was not home, probably playing with Eileen

Kreek or another friend. Jim and Carry are riding in a toy car. They are so cute and little.

In one picture, I am hugging Mom. I recently saw two young girls in church, around eight, sit with their mothers in the same manner. It must be a developmental stage that young girls pass through right before puberty.

Even playing, Carry was in a dress!

I felt a sharp pain when I looked at these happy family scenes. Tears came to my eyes. Mom looks so young, happy. Pictures taken just six months later would show a much older, sadder woman. Like a fortune teller with a crystal ball, I could see the future and know the tragic events that were getting ready to unfold for this family.

Mom, relaxed, and content with my antics.

EVERYTHING CHANGES

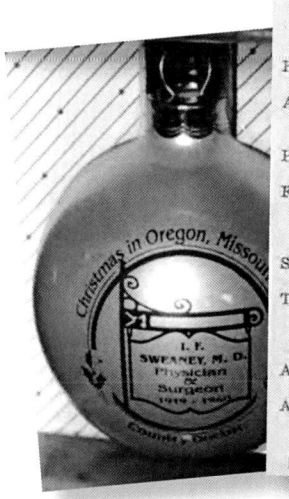

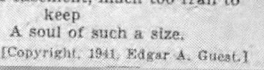

EULOGY

By EDGAR A. GUEST.

His weary body lies asleep
    Against life's endless din,
As if it was too frail to keep
    His restless spirit in.

He rushed through life so eagerly
    I think perhaps he knew,
For all the charms he wished
      to see
    His days would be too few.

So much he crowded in a day,
    So brave in doing good
That soon he would be called
      away,
    I think he understood.

And now at last in endless sleep
    His weary body lies;
A casement, much too frail to
      keep
    A soul of such a size.
[Copyright, 1941, Edgar A. Guest.]

BETTY MILLSON CALLED.

— Frank Sweaney, 1960

I do not remember Betty Millison. For me, she was just a seventy-year old woman who lived on a farm with her brother, Henry. She never married and kept house for both of them. For whatever reason, she was one of my dad's favorite patients. If I had to guess, she was probably a good cook and fed my dad treats. She died on July 2, 1960. I do not remember her, but her name will forever be engraved on my heart.

When people describe Dad in the later years of his life, it does not take a medical professional to know that he was becoming ill. Mary Kreek wrote that "Some evenings, after all patients had finally left, and he was very tired and already not well, Doc would sit down on the sofa and ask Mrs. Narans and me to sing hymns for him, which we gladly did. One of his favorite hymns was "The Old Rugged Cross."

His body was already beginning to shut down. The seven years of too little sleep, and his habit of fending off the exhaustion with sugar and caffeine, were catching up to him. I now know that he was suffering from a serious disease that medical science was just beginning to understand, malignant hypertension.

Dr. Jay Milne wrote me that he took Dad's blood pressure the summer of 1959. It was 247/120. To my lay ears that was a frightening number, but it was not until the late fifties that researchers began to prove the relationship between high blood pressure and heart and kidney failure. Dr. Milne noted that, "Of course, losing weight would have helped, but even so, this disease was very difficult to treat." New drugs were beginning to be released in 1960, but they were not widely available, or did not seem to be in rural areas. Perhaps the bottom line is that Doc took care of everyone but himself.

People close to Dad tried to help him. His staff would encourage patients to come during office hours. Yvonne remembered, "One time a couple was taking their evening drive after supper, and they stopped in the office to see Doc." Mrs. Narans recalled answering the phone at the office, and the woman on the other end asked, "Can Doc stop and see me on his way home from Fairfax Hospital?" Mrs. Narans asked if the patient couldn't come in that afternoon. She replied, "No, I'm going shopping in St. Joseph." Pat Kee remembers trying to screen calls to weed out less significant medical situations, but Dad would get upset if he found out that she had done so. He never wanted to turn anyone away. Phyllis Narans recalled, "He didn't know the word *no* or *no time* when it came to seeing patients. Many times Doc would be in the office until 10:00 p.m. and then begin making house calls while eating a candy bar or ring of bologna."

At home, Mom was trying to respond also. She stopped putting salt on the food. Medical science had not yet clearly associated sodium intake with high blood pressure, but Mom instinctively knew it was not healthy for Dad to eat salt-laden food. One Sunday, during a family gathering, my cousin Marilyn remembered my dad getting a call regarding a patient at Fairfax Hospital. My mom asked him if someone else could go. He was so tired. He said, "No, there is no one else." and left the family gathering.

Dad had established a pattern in his short time practicing medicine in Oregon and people grew accustomed to it. At first, it had probably been exciting and so rewarding. But he never developed the ability to set limits. His life was like a snowball going downhill. How do you stop it once it begins to pick up momentum? How do you re-invent a situation that is built around love and care? Phyllis told him when he was in the hospital that he would have to change his ways. He answered, "But Phil, what if that was the one time that I needed to go."

In May 1960, realizing he was very ill, Dad contacted a local insurance man. He purchased a top-of-the-line insurance policy to protect his family. A couple of weeks after his death, the local man made a very difficult trip to our house to return the premium that Dad had paid him. The policy could not go into effect since it had been purchased so recently. Mom did not contest the decision of the company.

By June, Dad had reached the point where he simply could not continue without medical attention for himself. Phyllis recalled that he was beginning to make mistakes with his patient care, and Mrs. Narans had to ask him "if that was really the treatment he wanted for a patient." Pat Kee remembered that he was vomiting blood in the small bathroom in the office. The noise reached her at her desk in the waiting room.

I remember Lou Ann crying the night Mom took Dad to the hospital in St. Joe. Mom led Dad to his car. That was the last time that I saw my dad. I vaguely remember seeing him in a wheel chair, but Lou Ann tells me that must be a dream. She says that we did not visit him.

Mom was at Dad's side during the next month. He was not allowed visitors. At first the town was in denial. When Mom told one of Dad's patients that the doctors said that he might not make it, the local man just looked at her not comprehending her words. It was during these last weeks of June, 1960, that the get-well cards started arriving. Janette and Sandy Dobbins placed a book at the Green Kitchen in Forest City in which people wrote notes. One group started collecting four-leaf clovers in a large jar to deliver to Dad.

I found a hand-written letter in Grandma McCluey's suitcase from grandmother Sweaney to her son. She started it by saying, "I am glad to hear that you are feeling better." I wonder who told Granny that piece of information. It must have been a casual statement only referring to how he felt better than the previous night or day. He was clearly not getting better.

Toward the middle of July, the town began to hold prayer vigils. Ruth Lippold wrote Mom, "The night we had a prayer vigil. We had it from 5:15 p.m. to 5:30 a.m. I asked that as the morning was opening like a flower bud, so might Doc Sweaney's [life]. Then after I heard he had come through the night, I again started building my foundation of hope."

Mom had heard the news that Betty Millison had died, but she had kept it to herself. One afternoon my mother sat watching my dad sleep. When he awoke, he said, "I dreamt Betty Millison called. She was going on a trip and wanted me to come with her." Mom knew then that Dad would not be returning home.

He died a short time later on July 18, 1960, my mom's 42nd birthday.

During those first months of intense grief and loneliness, Mom framed Dad's formal portrait. The picture had been reproduced and appeared beside obituaries printed in newspapers throughout Northwest Missouri. Behind the picture, she placed the folded letter from Baptist Memorial Hospital praising Dad's work as an intern in Memphis. She found this eulogy in a newspaper and tucked it along the edge of the picture. It must have comforted her.

I. Frank Sweaney 1919 -1960

EULOGY

By EDGAR A. GUEST.

His weary body lies asleep
  Against life's endless din,
As if it was too frail to keep
  His restless spirit in.

He rushed through life so eagerly
  I think perhaps he knew,
For all the charms he wished
      to see
  His days would be too few.

So much he crowded in a day,
  So brave in doing good
That soon he would be called
      away,
  I think he understood.

And now at last in endless sleep
  His weary body lies;
A casement, much too frail to
    keep
  A soul of such a size.

[Copyright. 1941. Edgar A. Guest.]

I See Snapshots In My Mind.

– Deborah Sweaney

The summer of 1960 was very hot. Homes were not air conditioned, and fans did little to cool the Missouri air. I was home alone with our house keeper, Dorothy Snider, when she received the call that Dad was dead. She did not say the words. Even so, as young as I was, I picked up something in her voice and knew Dad was gone. Within an hour our house was flooded with people. It had been so quiet that previous month. People had come and gone, paying little attention to the small children in the house. Out-of-town relatives used the house as a pit stop on their way to the hospital in St. Joe.

When my mother returned from the hospital this time, she seemed to be a very different person.

Very shortly, people started bringing food. For the longest time, I associated Jell-O salads with death. I have lived on the East coast for almost forty years, but I will always think of myself as a Midwesterner, and my way of responding to the world was created in that small Midwest Missouri town. I remember when I lived in Washington, D.C., a friend's husband died. I took baked chicken to the family. When someone asked me about it, I said, "I'm a Midwesterner, I bring food."

My memories of the next month, and maybe the next several years, appear in my mind like snapshots—not images from actual snapshots, but similar, as if I am flipping pages in an photograph album.

Me and Lou Ann in matching dresses for Dad's funeral; me, Mom, and Merrill and Berniece Ferguson in a large black car; our family sitting underneath a green canopy in the cemetery; Granny waving a funeral parlor fan—a paper picture of Jesus stapled to a wooden stick that did little to stir the air; the honor guard folding the American flag honoring Dad's World War II service that covered the casket; him walking over and handing the flag to Mom; our house full of people...

The church was so crowded the Missouri Highway patrol had to be called in to direct traffic.

Merrill Ferguson did not preach at Dad's funeral service. That would have been too hard for him. Instead, Mom chose Rev. Hagee from Mound City. He was not as close to our family and therefore a little more removed from the emotion of the day. I found a letter from Rev. Hagee in the suitcase refusing to take any money for performing the service.

While Mom was stoic, Grandma Sweaney cried. I realize that my emotional makeup is closer to Granny than to my mother's. I cry like her with noticeable sobs.

Twenty-nine years later cleaning out Mom's house after her funeral, we found that flag still folded in her dresser. We debated what to do with it. We four represent a spectrum of political viewpoints, all falling somewhere around that mythical center line. I fall on the right-hand side of it, Carry and Jim, somewhere around the middle, but Lou Ann, representative of her sixties generation and a Marin County California lifestyle, falls on the left. Jim, so reminiscent of

Dad, teased with a twinkle in his eyes: "We can't give it to Lou Ann. She might burn it."

Carry took the flag with her other items. I have since wondered how many white stars appear on its blue field. I do not know if that flag tucked away since the summer of 1960 had fifty white stars on its blue field or forty-eight. It is likely it only has forty-eight stars not yet reflecting the addition of Alaska and Hawaii.

Around the County . . .

Residents of Oregon and vicinity this week lost one of their most prominet citizens in the passing of Dr. I. F. Sweaney.

Dr. Sweaney gave his all—day in, day out; week in, week out—and had done so from the day he moved to Oregon to serve as a local physician.

Putting himself last, Dr. Sweaney was never too busy or too tired to answer any one's call day or night, regardless of weather conditions.

Dr. Sweaney, not only was unselfish, he was kind, generous faithful, and made each patien feel that there was hope. He had an unusual love for children. That fact remained on the walls of his office, where pictures of the babies he had delivered, and small children patients, hung by the hundreds.

With his passing, very few homes in the community remain untouched. He was indeed an honorable citizen, always devoted to his family, his profession and his patients.

Holt County Sentinel, July, 1960.

There are days that change the course of your life. One day the world is one way. The next day the world is different, never to be the same again. Sometimes the events of the day change a family's life. July 18, 1960, was such a day for me and my family. Dad's death changed everything.

Now I realize that for many in the small community of Holt County, Missouri, Doc Sweaney's death must have caused a big change in their lives. Doc had been there for them, night and day. He knew the right words to say. He teased, made them laugh, delivered bad news when he had to do so, but they knew he would be there to help. In July, 1960, this comforting presence, an integral part of their sense of community, of security, was gone.

My family, like the rest of the country, was glued to the television in November of 1963 after President Kennedy's assassination. I recall my mother's comment in watching Jacqueline Kennedy in her black mourning clothes with her two small children, John Jr. and Caroline, by her side: "I know just how she feels." Mom knew what it was to have to deal with the intense feeling of grief for the man you loved when the people surrounding you are grieving on a different level.

The community's sorrow is clear in the printed obituaries and notes in the local papers from that summer. Many of the very religious people turned to God to explain Dad's death. So many wrote Mom that they thought Dad was doing God's work. Grandma's suitcase full of sympathy cards and letters show the pain many felt.

That fall, the award-winning Oregon high school band performed a memorial concert in honor of Dad. He had taken care of so many of the young musicians through their childhood illnesses and accidents.

MEMORIES CARRIED FOR OVER FIFTY YEARS

Doc Sweaney's death was so sad. To me, it was like the Kennedy Assassination.

— Billie Bailey Banks, a few years older than me

The one thing I remember most was when your dad died very unexpectedly and young. I remember like it was yesterday, my mother crying when she got the news.

— Steve Burrier, my classmate

His untimely death broke every heart over on our hill.

— Arnie Kreek, my classmate

The county moved on but the people did not forget. Many, residents and former residents my age or older in 1960, have in their collection of memories a "Doc Sweaney story." Eileen Kreek wrote me:

I loved him. When I was eight years old, he did an appendectomy on me at the hospital in Fairfax. He stood on a wooden apple crate to be tall enough to reach the operating table. As I was being put to sleep, we sang "Mama's Little Baby Loves Shortnin' Bread" together. At least that is how I remember things.

When I called the Holt County Historical Society this year before returning to Missouri, the woman on the other end of the phone, a woman whose name I did not recognize, said "Oh, I remember Doc Sweaney. As a matter of fact, my mother and aunt were just talking and laughing about him over our holiday dinner this Christmas."

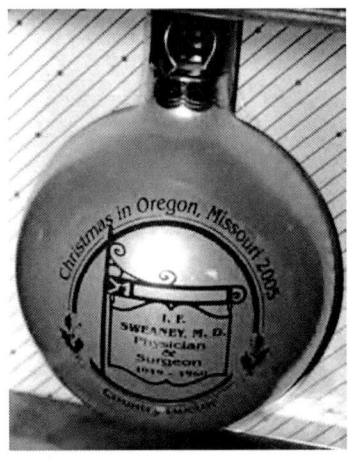

In the late 1990s, the town of Oregon started a tradition of creating Christmas ornaments to sell to support local charities. The first depicted local landmarks such as the old Courthouse. In 2005, forty-five years after his death, the town honored my father's memory with a Christmas ornament. It was their first to honor a person and the newspaper ran a series of articles about him.

PRETTY HARD YEAR.

— Iris McCluey Sweaney,
1981 remembering 1960

In Grandma's suitcase, I found my mother's handwritten obituary for her father. Grandpa McCluey died two weeks to the day after my father's funeral. In two weeks, my mother had gone from being my father's wife to my father's widow and then a father-less daughter. She now had four small children to support by herself. Lou Ann was eleven, I had just turned eight, Jim was four, and Carry was not yet two. The sense of grief in our house was palpable. Laughter which had been so central to life with my father left our home for years leaving in its place an overwhelming feeling of sadness.

In 1981, Mom wrote to my sister Carry about that devastating year, 1960. Her words were understated but I can feel her loss:

Aunt Maude's son-in-law (Ross Pyatt) died the same week your daddy did. Harold McCluey (my cousin), Uncle Will, Aunt Maude, your daddy, your grandpa and Ross Pyatt, all died in less than 10 months. Pretty hard year.

I do not know how my mother did it but she moved through those years. I figure that she felt she had no choice. Iris McCluey Sweaney just persevered.

My mother above all else was practical. She had a business to close. She worked with Pat Kee to reconcile my father's business records. Many patients still had outstanding medical bills. Some were never collected. Mom, like so many women of her generation, hadn't paid much attention to the family finances. The new circumstances required that she do so. One of her first acts was to have Francis Jackson take my father's Oldsmobile to a car auction.

She moved the many file cabinets that contained my father's medical records to the second floor of our house. They took up most of the room on the landing. Law mandated that the records be saved for at least seven years before they could be destroyed. The cabinets were full of patient folders, x-rays, and EKG strips. Thus, every time we went to our bedrooms we were reminded of my father's medical practice.

My mother brought other items home. We were the only family I knew that, in addition to a hammer and a screwdriver, had a hemostat as a basic part of the family toolset. We found that this delicate instrument designed to stop bleeding by clamping veins was perfect for many basic household tasks such as de-clogging drains. It became a family joke that we should get the hemostat and "heme it."

My mother also brought home my father's large black safe. I can still picture Jim holding one of my father's stethoscopes up to the safe trying to listen for clicks that would help him pick the lock. He had seen master criminals on television use this technique for safe cracking. He was never able to open the safe using the medical instrument. I am relieved that he did not succeed, it might have led to a life of crime...

Mom had a mission. Her children were going to get a college education. She started a small home-based kindergarten. In the mid-1960s when Lyndon Johnson's Great Society programs for education brought the kindergarten into the public school system, my mother was forced to shut down her small business, and went to work as a school aide. The aide job was never a happy fit for my mother. The pecking order meant that she had playground duty which she hated. In 1969, due to health reasons, she left the public school system.

In 1970, ten years after Dad's death, Mom took a major leap and decided to run for political office. She entered the race for Holt County Tax Collector on the Republican ticket. She campaigned for the job driving over county roads that my dad had travelled ten years earlier on house calls. She was welcomed in the farm houses. Over coffee, she discussed Dad with people who still loved him. Her campaign advertisements paid for by "Friends of Iris Sweaney" reminded voters that she was my father's widow. She won the position of Holt County Tax Collector decisively.

Mom shocked the members of the First Christian Church early in her first term as collector. The minister was talking about Matthew, the "publican tax collector of the New Testament." He said, "No one liked tax collectors." From her place in the second row of the north side of the church, Mom spoke, "And they still don't." People looked around not believing that those words had come from my mother. To speak aloud during the sermon was not done, and for Mom to do so was uncharacteristic, so counter to their image of the dedicated, widowed, Sunday school teacher.

During the next four years, Mom grew in confidence and independence. She was now in her fifties. She proved to be an able administrator. When she ran for re-election she gained more votes than any other candidate on the local ticket. This time *Iris Sweaney* was elected, not Doc's widow.

Mom had another side to her that she did not often show. Some place in the boxes of Bailey family mementoes is a picture. In it, Mom is clinging to a teen-aged Bert Bailey, on the back of his motorcycle. Bert had attended my mother's home-based kindergarten and had been one of her favorite students. He had pulled up to his house as my mother prepared to leave after a campaign visit with his mother, Bonnie. He said, "Mrs. Sweaney, do you want a ride?" To everyone's surprise, she jumped on the back. I wish I had a copy of that photograph for my own collection.

She retired from the court house after twelve years as tax collector. By this time, we had all graduated from college. She began to relax. She spent hours in her garden, growing vegetables and canning the tomatoes and green beans. She also nurtured many of the young children in the neighborhood, reading books to them, and putting band aids on their scrapes.

The church was crowded for her funeral in 1989. The family gathered at the church for a lunch before the service that was, of course, provided by the church ladies. I had been married to my husband for about a year and half. He had never experienced small town life and was unprepared for a funeral service that brought out half the town. I tried to explain to him that small towns honored their dead. I told him that this one was nothing like my father's funeral when the state police were called in to direct traffic.

I was reminded that in Oregon there is a defined etiquette to funerals, a schedule to the grieving process. On the night before a funeral there is an open casket viewing. So, many came to the funeral home to console us. We had all arrived from our homes located in states far away and were greeted by people who had played a role in our childhood. So many started the conversation with "Let me tell you a story about your father." At first, I was upset since it was my mother that we were mourning not my father. Now, I understand that is one of the ways people cope with death: They remember the past and it helps them with the grief of the present.

Mom's unwavering faith told her that she and Dad would be reunited in heaven. Lou Ann dreamt of Mom during the week we closed her house. In her dream, Mom came to her in a beautiful apricot flowing peignoir set. She looked so pretty and happy in the apricot color. Lou Ann asked, "Mom, have you found Dad yet?"

Mom, not a bit worried, knowing she would find him, answered, "No, you know there are a lot of people up here."

I like that image of heaven. Mom and Dad are reunited. They continue their love story. But, this time, Mom gets to establish a slower pace.

I have always thought that my mother's life was not easy. Her young years were marked by poverty, and she always felt at the bottom of her small town's social ladder. She dropped out of college to put her husband through medical school, only to see him die on her 42nd birthday after just eight years of practice. In her middle years, she was left to raise four small children by herself. Looking back, I can now see that at times she suffered from depression and anxiety.

Yet, we discovered in her papers a document that she had written on her 65th birthday. It is a beautiful testimony to the joys and challenges of her life. There is absolutely no sense of bitterness or regret. Each time I read it, I am moved. I have shared it with church groups when I have been called to lead devotions, as one of the most beautiful statements of faith I have ever read.

July 18, 1983

Things I am thankful
for on my 65th Birthday

For telephone calls from Lou
Ann and Tory. Cora, Hannah
and Joshua from Cora at
their Mother's house. From
Debby, Gwen and Maxine
Edwards (who never forgets).
For a bountiful garden and
the good health to work in
it. For the beautiful card
and call from Avis. For a
cool evening to sit in the
yard with a beautiful half
moon over the pine tree.
For the absence of mosquitoes
even after such a wet spring
and early summer. For more
fireflies than I have seen for
years. For beautiful memories

July 18, 1983

Things I am thankful for on my 65th Birthday.

For telephone calls from Lou Ann and Tory. Hannah, and Joshua [and] from Oona at their Mother's house. From Debby, Gwen, and Maxine Edwards (who never forgets). For a bountiful garden and the good health to work in it. For the beautiful card and call from Avis. For a cool evening to sit in the yard with a beautiful half moon over the pine tree. For the absence of mosquitoes even after such a wet spring and early summer. For more fireflies than I have seen for years. For beautiful memories of Frank who has been gone twenty three years today. So much of his strength of will has "rubbed off" on me making it possible for me to face the many problems of these years of carrying on alone. For the twelve years work at the Court House which not only provided financial security but was a great learning experience for me. For a great family — I wish for them each a long and successful life. Most of all for a loving God who has made all this possible.

of Frank who has been gone twenty-three years today. So much of his strength of will has "rubbed off" on me and making it possible for me to face the many problems of these years of carrying on alone. For the twelve years work at the Court House which not only provided financial security but was a great learning experience for me. For a great family - I wish for them a long and successful life. Most of all for a loving God who has made all this possible.

EPILOGUE

Lou Ann, Jim, Carry and I have long since left Oregon. There are no longer any Sweaneys left in our small town and fewer and fewer of the people of my memories. Lou Ann and Carry both live with their families in California, Lou Ann in Marin County, north of San Francisco, and Carry in San Jose. Jim and his wife have settled in Charlotte, N.C. In 2006, after living for over thirty years in the Washington, D.C. area, I moved with my husband, Jim, to Carlisle, Pennsylvania.

Carlisle is in the Cumberland Valley. I recently drove through the mountains, part of the Appalachian chain that protects the valley on both sides, and had such a feeling of nostalgia. The scenery very much reminded me of the Ozark Mountains, and I recalled family trips to visit Granny Sweaney.

I have returned from my journey to my childhood triggered by that old suitcase. I have cried but I also laughed. My New York City born and bred husband cannot really identify with my emotion of returning to my home state. He did get some "husband-points" by saying he thought it was endearing.

At first, I thought I might write about how much has changed since my youth, how rural America is in crisis. I even thought that it would be interesting to focus on the theme of Holt County between the two floods, 1952 and 2011. I considered discussing the changes in health care in the last decades, how different from the days when my father practiced medicine. The world has moved so far. Life is so different.

Instead, my story became a memoir, an attempt to capture my youth and to remember my parents. I see so much of both my mother and my father in me, strengths, flaws, and weaknesses from each. Somehow our creator used the miracle of genetics to combine the Sweaney-McCluey genes to form a unique person, Deborah.

Sometimes I do question the wisdom that gave me my father's inclination toward obesity and only a little of his charisma, and put just a few of Grandma McCluey's creative genes in my DNA. However, I also got my love of history from my mother. She could recite in order the Kings of Judea and Israel in the divided Kingdom of the Old Testament and what happened in each of their reigns. Oh, I wish for more of her strength. God made McCluey women so strong.

On particularly intense mornings, I look down at the large number of empty cans of Diet Coke beside my desk and think of my father. I know how easy it is to let drive and energy overtake me and cease to serve me well.

My roots remain deep in the soil of Missouri. As I look out my window at the beautiful Pennsylvania mountains that guard my valley, I think of the words of the psalmist, "I will lift up mine eyes unto the hills, from whence cometh my help" and am filled with appreciation for the beauty of my adopted state. I have moved on from my childhood, but sometimes I am called from a land that is bordered by a wide muddy river with a personality of its own.

Tomorrow, I will put the cards, letters, and pictures back in Grandma McCluey's suitcase. My extra bedroom needs to resurface as a guest room. I feel ready to pack up my past, but I will carry it with me. My memories no longer focus on the pain of Dad's death but are now balanced with love and the sound of laughter.

Pine Tree in Welty Park, Oregon, Missouri

In 1953, the Adelpha Club made scrapbooks for children to read in Dad's waiting room. In appreciation, Dad gave a seedling to be planted at Welty Park. The tall tree now stands as a living memorial to the doctor who loved and was loved by this community.

NOTES

HOLT COUNTY, 1952

Hearthstone Legacy Publications produces a great CD full of Holt County history and maps including the 1950 map from the Missouri State Highway Commission and the complete 1882 History of Holt and Atchison Counties, Missouri, by the National Historical Publishing Company. I recommend the CD for anyone interested in the history of Northwest Missouri.

Two local Holt County writers have created great resources on Holt County history. Gone Home by Eileen Deer documents the lives of people buried in Holt County cemeteries and includes information on Annie Ben Hayes. The 150 Years of Forest City, Missouri, by Margaret Ann Edwards contains an account of the once booming city of Forest City and the floods on the Missouri River.

Holt County Sentinels were made available for research by the Holt County Historical Society.

Undaunted Courage by Stephen Ambrose tells the story of the Lewis and Clark journey up the Missouri and their reaction to the beauty north of Kansas City, present day Holt County.

George Fitch wrote of the "The Missouri River: Its Habits and Eccentricities Described by a Personal Friend." in the April 1907 edition of the American Magazine. (Vol. 53, No. 6)

An account of the flood of 1952 including the quote by General Shingler can be found can be on the website:

http://siouxcityjournal.com/news/article_f277abc1-c299-5b4a-90fe-398b6bf27575.html

HEALTH CARE (FIFTIES STYLE)

Polio: An American Story by David M. Oshinsky and Paralyzing Fear, The Story of Polio in America, an Emmy award winning documentary, cover the impact polio had on lives of Americans and the fear it generated. Websites also provided information on the disease including the support for the March of Dimes by celebrities such as Elvis Presley:

http://americanhistory.si.edu/polio   http://www.elvisinfonet.com/interview_joannekelly.html

The Treatment of Hypertension: A Story of Myths, Misconceptions, Controversies and Heroics by Marvin Moser, M.D. is the source for the information on the disease and the quote from the American Heart Association position paper can be found on page 27.

Statistics on diseases in Missouri in 1953 were provided by the Bureau of Communicable Disease Control and Prevention, Missouri Department of Health and Senior Services.

The Green County Medical Society offers cassette tapes of Singing Doctor songs and granted permission to quote the lyrics. All proceeds from the songs go to the Singing Doctor Scholarship Endowment Fund at the University of Missouri Medical School.

LIFE IN RURAL AMERICA

Life with Dick and Jane and Friends stories were reissued by Pearson Scott Foresman in 1993.

The Church in the Wildwood was written by Dr. William S. Pitts in 1857 and is often referred to as "The Little Brown Church."

ABOUT THE AUTHOR

Deborah Sweaney lives in Carlisle, Pennsylvania. Farther away from her roots in Missouri than she might like, but the Pennsylvania hills carry a familiarity reminiscent of the Ozarks. And it is not too far from New York City, where her husband, Jim, grew up. Jim, she remarks, "never can quite grasp my childhood." She moved to Washington D.C. just after college to intern for Missouri Representative Jerry Litton, and Washington remained her home for the next thirty years. She worked for multiple government agencies including an internship with the planning organization for the Nixon Presidential Library, the White House Office of Records Management, and finally with the Federal Deposit Insurance Corporation (FDIC). She and her husband left Washington, D.C. for Carlisle, PA. in 2006. In her words, "After 9/11 the security in the city was so overwhelming, it no longer seemed like fun to be there."

Ms. Sweaney's interest in family history extends beyond the personal. In 2010 she established her own company, Ancestry Searches, which specializes in on-line searches to unlock the treasures, or solve the mysteries of any family's past. She has worked with several families to write their family histories and inspires people to explore their own unique heritage. She is a member of several professional associations dedicated to the study of history and is on the governing body of First Presbyterian of Carlisle, a 275-year old historic church where she developed an oral history program for the congregation. In addition, she is a former adjunct instructor at Messiah College, the University of the District of Columbia, and Marymount University in Arlington, Va., and has been a consultant for National History Day.

"When I lecture on family research and genealogy, I am frequently introduced as being from Washington, D.C. But, I don't think of myself that way. I know I will always be Debby Sweaney from Oregon, Missouri."

WA